'John Quiggin is the intellectual equivalent of a dazzling fireworks display. I walk away from every encounter with a bright new insight, and this book is no exception. Agree or disagree, Professor Quiggin is a veritable trove of fresh insights.

'Spanning nearly four decades, this volume brings together some of Professor Quiggin's most provocative contributions, driven by a deep commitment to equity. It will pique your curiosity and encourage you to work towards a better world.'

Andrew Leigh, Parliamentarian and author
of *The Shortest History of Economics*

AFTER NEOLIBERALISM

AFTER NEOLIBERALISM

JOHN QUIGGIN

Australian
National
University

ANU PRESS

GLOBAL THINKERS SERIES

ANU PRESS

Published by ANU Press
The Australian National University
Canberra ACT 2600, Australia
Email: anupress@anu.edu.au

Available to download for free at press.anu.edu.au

ISBN (print): 9781760466510
ISBN (online): 9781760466527

WorldCat (print): 1434597312
WorldCat (online): 1434597367

DOI: 10.22459/AN.2024

Cover design and layout by ANU Press

This book is published under the aegis of the Public Policy editorial board of ANU Press.

Contents

List of tables

Acknowledgements

Over a career of more than 40 years, the people who have helped me in various ways are too numerous to list. Any such list would certainly omit many to whom I owe a debt of gratitude. I must, however, thank my wife and long-term colleague, Nancy Wallace, who edited many of the papers collected here and provided invaluable research support, as well as the love and kindness that has carried me this far.

I also thank Andrew Kennedy of The Australian National University (ANU) for the initiative of producing this volume, ANU Publication Subsidy Fund for supporting it, and Glenine Hamlyn for the editorial work needed to turn a disparate collection of articles into a coherent volume.

Abbreviations

ABS	Australian Bureau of Statistics
ACCC	Australian Competition and Consumer Commission
ACTU	Australian Council of Trade Unions
AIPS	Australian Institute of Political Science
ALP	Australian Labor Party
ASEAN	Association of Southeast Asian Nations
COAG	Council of Australian Governments
DSGE	dynamic stochastic general equilibrium [theory]
ECB	European Central Bank
EU	European Union
4DW Global	4 Day Week Global
GFC	Global Financial Crisis
the Depression	the Great Depression
GDP	gross domestic product
GMI	guaranteed minimum income
GNP	gross national product
GST	goods and services tax
ICT	information and communications technology
IPOs	initial public offerings
IMF	International Monetary Fund
MTAWE	Male Total Average Weekly Earnings
MFP	multifactor productivity
NCC	National Competition Council

NCP	National Competition Policy
New Protection	New Protection policy
NIT	negative income tax
OECD	Organisation for Economic Co-operation and Development
OPEC	Organization of the Petroleum Exporting Countries
the Accord	Prices and Incomes Accord
Trade Practices Act	*Trade Practices Act 1974*
UBI	universal basic income
UK	United Kingdom
UNCTAD	United Nations Conference on Trade and Development
US	of the United States of America (used adjectivally)
USA	United States of America
VAT	Value Added Tax
Virgin	Virgin Blue
White Australia	the White Australia policy
White Paper	White Paper on Full Employment in Australia 1945
Work Choices	Work Choices (legislation)

Introduction

Since we emerged from the lockdown phase of the COVID-19 pandemic that began in 2020, it is clear that something important has changed. Old certitudes about work and life, government and politics, and the way the economy works were being questioned even before the pandemic. Now they appear to have collapsed altogether.

The contrast between our current situation and that at the turn of the 21st century is startling. As the sun rose on New Year's Day 2000 and it became apparent that the much-predicted 'Millennium Bug' had failed to bite, the world seemed to have entered a new era of capitalist prosperity. That new era had been prophesied in numerous writings, ranging from academic works such as Francis Fukuyama's *The End of History* (1992) to airport bestsellers like Thomas Friedman's *The Lexus and the Olive Tree* (1999).

Many terms have been used to describe the set of ideas and policies that held sway at the beginning of the 21st century.

In most cases, these terms were initially positive or neutral, but they became primarily pejorative over time. This reflects the fact that critics of a ruling ideology need terms to describe it. By contrast, those who accept and implement such an ideology rarely see it as such.

Terms used to describe the newly dominant ideology included 'economic rationalism', the 'Washington Consensus' and 'market liberalism'. Political and economic commentators finally settled on 'neoliberalism'.

As is usual with any widely invoked political concept (for example, 'democracy' or 'socialism'), the term neoliberalism has been used and misused in many different ways. The range of different uses of 'neoliberalism' has led some (primarily supporters of neoliberal ideas) to suggest that the term is nothing more than a slur, applicable to anything left-wingers dislike.

But it is still true, as US Supreme Court Justice Potter Stewart famously said of obscenity, that even if we can't define neoliberalism precisely, we can recognise it when we see it. Properly understood, it is the ideological underpinning of the era of financialised capitalism that emerged from the economic crises of the early 1970s and remained dominant for the rest of the 20th century.

The central idea of neoliberalism was that markets, particularly financial markets, generally outperform governments in the allocation of resources and investments. Neoliberalism came in a variety of forms, reflecting the variety of liberalism itself, but was different from preceding forms of liberalism because of the need to respond to the successes and failures of social democracy in the second half of the 20th century. In one form or another, neoliberalism became the unquestioned basis for the thinking of both centre-right and centre-left parties around the world.

My own academic career has coincided almost exactly with the era of neoliberalism. My first journal article was published in 1979, the year Margaret Thatcher became prime minister of the United Kingdom (UK) and inaugurated the program of radical reform that became known as Thatcherism. I began work on this retrospective volume in late 2022, just after Liz Truss ended her brief and disastrous stint in the same position. Her sole accomplishment in that period was to demonstrate that a Thatcherite policy program was no longer acceptable, even to financial markets.

Between those endpoints, neoliberalism surged around the world, taking different forms in different countries and reaching a triumphal high point in the 1990s. Successive financial disasters, culminating in the Global Financial Crisis (GFC) of 2008, discredited the central ideas underlying neoliberalism. However, these ideas remained part of the mental equipment of the political and policymaking classes. As soon as the immediate crisis was over, neoliberalism re-emerged in zombie form,[1] driving disastrous policies of austerity that produced a decade of miserable economic performance throughout the capitalist world.

It is only in the last five years or so that new thinking has begun to fill the gap left by the failure of neoliberalism. Ideas like universal basic income, a four-day working week and autonomous remote work have moved from

---

1   My book *Zombie Economics: How Dead Ideas Still Walk Among Us* (Quiggin 2010) developed this trope, describing the life cycle of zombie ideas, from birth through life and death to reanimation in undead form.

the margins to the centre of the policy debate. The movement towards gender equity has extended to encompass measures including parental leave and expanded provision of childcare. Privatisation has been replaced by an expansion of public enterprise in a variety of fields. Serious efforts are finally being made to bring global financial markets under control.

Over the 40 years of neoliberalism, I have written hundreds of journal articles, book chapters and opinion pieces presenting a critical view of the dominant ideology and, more recently, advocating alternatives. In this book, I have picked a representative selection of these, running from the 1990s to the last couple of years.

The book is organised as follows.

Chapter 1, originally published in 1987, was my first venture into the public debate over productivity and economic growth. It was published in the *Current Affairs Bulletin*, a peer-reviewed journal produced by the Workers Educational Association. The journal made valuable contributions to Australian public debate from its inception in 1947 until 1998. The gap created by its departure has been filled by online publications, most notably *The Conversation*.

The article was a response to a string of jeremiads put out by supporters of what came to be known as 'micro-economic reform', predicting economic disaster if the policies they proposed were not implemented. The supposed poor performance of the Australian economy relative to that of Japan was of particular concern.

My central observation, repeated in different forms in much of my subsequent work, was that the supposed decline of Australia's relative living standards was largely a statistical illusion, and that the apocalyptic scenarios in which Australians were doomed to become the 'white trash of Asia'[2] were unlikely to eventuate.

Rereading the article after nearly 40 years, I would change almost nothing. I have deleted two figures that I could no longer reproduce from the available data and that added nothing to the analysis.

---

2   As Dobell (2015) observes in relation to the 'white trash of Asia' catchphrase, 'Pinning down great quotes can be an experience as ephemeral and exasperating as hunting the snark.' Nevertheless, Dobell ultimately attributes the phrase to Lee Kuan Yew, former prime minister of Singapore.

Chapter 2 is a retrospective, examining the rise and decline of neoliberalism from the 1970s to the COVID-19 pandemic. I present a 'three-party' model, in which the main movements driving contemporary politics are categorised as neoliberal (soft or hard), Trumpist[3] and leftist. In conclusion, I discuss the requirements for a successful left response to the crisis and offer some suggestions for a way forward.

Chapter 3, drawn from my 1996 book, *Great Expectations*, turns the focus back to Australia. I describe the background of Australian neoliberalism (referred to at the time as 'economic rationalism' or 'micro-economic reform'). The growth of the state from the Second World War to the Whitlam government is contrasted with the subsequent retreat under Fraser, Hawke and Keating. The chapter ends with a discussion of the National Competition Policy, which turned out to be the last major instalment of micro-economic reform.

Chapter 4, written for the Committee for Economic Development of Australia and published in their journal *Growth,* deals with what is arguably the most distinctively neoliberal policy project, that of privatisation. The Thatcher government, in particular, focussed heavily on reversing the growth of public enterprise that had taken place over the course of the 20th century. By 2002, when this chapter was written, the project was running out of steam. The promised benefits of privatisation had not been delivered, and new privatisation proposals were facing increased opposition. My article proposed a revival of the concept of the mixed economy, in which both privatisation and nationalisation were available as policies to achieve an appropriate balance between the public and private sectors. Twenty years later, with large-scale Australian government initiatives in telecommunications and energy infrastructure, including the National Broadband Network (NBN) and public investment in renewable energy, such a policy seems to be emerging.

Chapter 5, first published in *The Economic and Labour Relations Review,* was notable at the time for treating neoliberal micro-economic reform as a policy agenda with a fixed beginning and end. Most commentators agree that micro-economic reform in Australia began with the floating of the dollar by the Hawke government in 1983. When the chapter was originally

---

3   I formerly used the term 'tribalist', which is unsatisfactory in various ways, as is Piketty's 'nativism'. Donald Trump leads and exemplifies the political tendency I am talking about, so 'Trumpist populism' seems the best term to describe it.

published, the dominant assumption was that 'reform'[4] was essential and would continue indefinitely. By contrast, I argued that the process had already ended with the introduction of the goods and services tax (GST) in 2000 and that, for the most part, the reform agenda had been exhausted. Over time, this latter point has become conventional wisdom. Calls for a return to 'reform' are obligatory in various contexts but are no longer taken seriously by anyone.

The main point of the chapter was that the benefits of reform had been oversold in various respects. Most relevantly to contemporary debates, I stressed the role of unsustainable increases in working hours and work intensity as a driver of the brief and illusory 'productivity miracle' of the early 1990s. In the wake of the pandemic lockdowns, issues of this kind are coming to the fore, with the rise of remote work and calls for a four-day standard working week.

Chapter 6, first published in the *Australian Economic Review*, was written in the aftermath of the GFC and summarised the key arguments of my book, *Zombie Economics: How Dead Ideas Still Walk Among Us*. I argued that the crisis provided sufficient evidence to reject the dominant models in academic macro-economics and finance theory, as well as policy claims such as the 'trickle-down' hypothesis and the case for comprehensive privatisation. In reality, few of these lessons were learned, and much of the policy response to the crisis has been irrelevant or counterproductive. As a result, we have learned some unflattering lessons about the economics profession, including policymakers, commentators, central bankers and academic economists.

In Chapter 7, which is based on a paper presented to a Reserve Bank conference, I return to the topic of productivity growth. By the time the paper was presented in 2011, it was clear that the supposed 'productivity miracle' of the 1990s was, at best, a temporary blip, and that all the measured gains had subsequently been lost. By this time, Australians recognised that calls for 'reform' and 'improved productivity' were little more than code words for 'work harder with fewer resources, and produce more'. As these calls were increasingly ignored, work intensity declined, and productivity slowed. In further writing, not included in this volume, I made the case that productivity growth in Australia is mainly driven by improvements

---

4   The word 'reform' is frequently used with a positive connotation, implicitly assuming that change is beneficial. However, this usage requires some level of agreement on the desirable direction of change. I use it to mean simply 'a change in form', without any implication as to the desirability of that change.

in information and communications technology (Quiggin 2017; 2018). Since we import most of the associated equipment, technological progress is manifested in improved terms of trade rather than measured multifactor productivity. The main lesson from this analysis is that Australian workers increasingly value work–life balance over increasing material living standards.

Chapter 8, based on an article in a special issue of *Politics & Society*, deals with the rise of financial markets to dominate the global economy in the era of neoliberalism. I contrast the adulation accorded to the 'Masters of the Universe' in the 1990s with the disastrous reality of the Global Financial Crisis and offer a number of suggestions for constraining the size and activity of the financial sector.

Chapters 9 and 10, written as the era of neoliberalism was drawing to a close, look forward rather than backward to possibilities for radical, even utopian change.

Chapter 9 deals with the idea of a universal basic income (UBI) and advocates what has been called a Livable Income Guarantee (Quiggin, Klein, and Henderson 2020). The central idea is to approach a UBI by focussing initially on extending a livable income to larger groups of people. This would be done by raising inadequate benefits like JobSeeker to a livable level and expanding eligibility to support activities such as volunteering. This 'Basic first' approach may be contrasted with a 'Universal first' approach of making a payment to everyone in the population but setting it at a level insufficient to support a living standard above the poverty line.

Chapter 10 presents arguments for a four-day standard working week. Working arrangements of many kinds were upended by the COVID pandemic. This experience showed that different ways of working were possible, notably including remote work. More broadly, the experience of the pandemic has restarted debates about reducing standard working hours that have been frozen under neoliberalism. Standard working hours fell steadily from 1850 to the 1980s but have been virtually unchanged since then. A four-day week is long overdue.

Bibliography

Dobell, Graeme. 2015. 'Lee Kuan Yew, Australia and "white trash"'. *Australian Journal of International Affairs* 69: 363–72.

Friedman, Thomas. 1999. *The Lexus and the Olive Tree: Understanding Globalization*. New York: Farrar, Strauss and Giroux.

Fukuyama, Francis. 1992. *The End of History and the Last Man*. New York: The Free Press.

Quiggin, John. 2010. *Zombie Economics: How Dead Ideas Still Walk Among Us*. Paperback Edition. Princeton: Princeton University Press. doi.org/10.1515/9781400842087.

Quiggin, John. 2017. 'The Productivity Commission's Multi-factor Problem'. *Inside Story*. 31 October 2017. insidestory.org.au/the-productivity-commissions-multi-factor-problem/.

Quiggin, John. 2018. 'The Not-So-Strange Death of Multifactor Productivity Growth'. *Australian Economic Review* 51, no. 2: 269–75. doi.org/10.1111/1467-8462.12275.

Quiggin, John, Elise Klein, and Troy Henderson. 2020. 'Meet the Liveable Income Guarantee: A Budget-ready Proposal That Would Prevent Unemployment Benefits Falling off a Cliff'. *The Conversation*. 1 October 2020. theconversation.com/meet-the-liveable-income-guarantee-a-budget-ready-proposal-that-would-prevent-unemployment-benefits-falling-off-a-cliff-146990.

1

White trash of Asia?

First published in 1987 as Quiggin, John. 'White Trash of Asia'. *Current Affairs Bulletin* 64: 18–25.[1]

Introduction

In recent years it has often been claimed that in the absence of radical changes in economic policies and social attitudes, Australians will soon be the 'poor white trash' of South-East Asia. The phrase itself appears to be due to Sir Roderick Carnegie, chairman of the mining company Conzinc RioTinto Australia, but other commentators ranging from Max Walsh, editor of the *Australian Financial Review*, to Lee Kuan Yew, prime minister of Singapore from 1959 to 1990, have made the same general claim.[2] In 1984, the claim was the subject of a conference of the Australian Institute of Political Science (AIPS), whose proceedings have recently been published as *Poor Nation of the Pacific?: Australia's Future?* (Scutt 1985).

The basis of the claim is the fact that, since about 1870, when Australia's income per capita was the highest in the world, Australia's rate of growth in per capita gross national product (GNP) has been slower than that of most other nations, with the result that we have fallen to about twelfth on the international ladder (depending on how the measurements are made).

1   I wish to thank Pat Quiggin for extensive help with the provision and interpretation of demographic data, and Bruce Chapman, Steve Dowrick, Fred Gruen and Tom Nguyen for useful discussions on the issues examined here. None of these should be assumed to share the views expressed here.
2   As noted in the Introduction, subsequent analysis has suggested that Lee Kuan Yew was probably the first to use the term.

This relatively poor performance is illustrated by statistics such as those in Tables 1.1–1.3. Table 1.1 (taken from Hughes 1985) illustrates the relative per capita GDP of Australia and other developed nations over the period 1870–1976. At least at first sight, it gives evidence of a dramatic decline in Australia's relative standard of living. Table 1.2 (taken from Dowrick and Nguyen 1986) gives more estimates of per capita GDP for the countries of the Organisation for Economic Co-operation and Development (OECD) over the postwar period.

Table 1.1 Relative GDP per capita (USA=100)

Country	Year						Growth rate	
	1870	1890	1913	1929	1960	1976	GDP	GDP p. cap.
Australia	173	145	107	74	75	80	3.2	1.1
Austria	53	58	48	54	69	2.6	2.1	NA
Belgium	123	104	82	75	66	84	2.1	1.5
Canada	80	77	81	70	78	91	3.8	2.0
Denmark	69	66	73	64	66	76	2.9	1.9
Finland	52	42	41	39	54	71	3.1	2.2
France	87	71	67	66	67	87	2.2	1.9
Germany	68	60	58	51	70	81	2.5	2.0
Italy	69	46	42	37	43	53	2.3	1.6
Japan	35	33	29	32	35	77	3.8	2.6
Netherlands	123	87	69	70	69	80	2.7	1.4
Norway	63	52	47	50	65	85	2.9	2.1
Sweden	54	48	55	61	79	88	3.0	2.3
Switzerland	104	88	74	85	85	78	2.4	1.6
UK	103	81	67	70	67	124	1.8	1.3
USA	100	100	100	100	100	100	3.5	1.9

Source: OECD

The main interest of these type of data for advocates of the white trash thesis is the relative ranking of different nations, and, here again, Australia seems to have performed poorly. By contrast, over about the last 30 years, the nations of South-East Asia have enjoyed very rapid growth in per capita incomes. Obviously, if these trends are extrapolated, these nations will, at some point, overtake us. Hughes (1985) has undertaken such an extrapolation, and the results are presented in Table 1.3.

Table 1.2 OECD per capita GDP levels (in 1975 $US) and rankings

	1950/52		1960		1973		1985	
1	USA	4748	USA	5195	USA	7480	USA	8709
2	Canada	3736	Switzerland	4424	Canada	6702	Canada	8037
3	Luxembourg	3474	Luxembourg	4239	Switzerland	6454	Sweden	7741
4	Switzerland	3295	Sweden	4160	Sweden	6407	Norway	7668
5	Australia	3216	Canada	4079	Luxembourg	6383	Denmark	7524
6	Sweden	3206	Australia	3894	Denmark	6205	Germany	7437
7	NZ	2897	Denmark	3761	Germany	5914	Luxembourg	7270
8	Denmark	2825	Germany	3711	France	5777	Japan	7019
9	UK	2773	NZ	3424	Australia	5745	Switzerland	6911
10	Belgium	2512	UK	3388	Belgium	5471	Australia	6891
11	Norway	2456	Netherlands	3198	Netherlands	5314	France	6890
12	Iceland	2320	Norway	3163	Iceland	5164	Finland	6621
13	Netherlands	2315	France	3163	Finland	5129	Austria	6545
14	France	2314	Iceland	3096	Norway	5052	Belgium	6441
15	Finland	2097	Belgium	3085	Japan	5025	Netherlands	5864
16	Germany	2059	Finland	2912	Austria	4837	Iceland	5594
17	Austria	1763	Austria	2764	UK	4709	UK	5390
18	Ireland	1560	Italy	2313	NZ	4681	NZ	5058
19	Italy	1470	Ireland	1868	Italy	3971	Italy	4818

#	1950/52		1960		1973		1985	
20	Spain	1304	Spain	1737	Spain	3841	Spain	4457
21	Japan	934	Greece	1674	Greece	3334	Greece	3981
22	Greece	900	Ireland	1385	Ireland	3038	Ireland	3546
23	Portugal	804	Portugal	1137	Portugal	2615	Portugal	3102
24	Turkey	796	Turkey	1044	Turkey	1586	Turkey	2361

Source: Dowrick and Nguyen (1986)

Table 1.3 Projections of GDP (1981)

	GDP 1981 (US$ billion)	GDP growth 1971–81 (% p.a.)	GDP[a] 2011 (projected, US$ billion)	GDP[b] 2031 (projected, US$ billion)
Indonesia	85	7.8	809	3632
Malaysia	25	7.8	236	1059
Philippines	39	6.2	236	787
Singapore	13	8.5	149	763
Thailand	37	7.2	296	1190
Total	**199**	**NA**	**1726**	**7431**
Australia	171	3.3	453	867

Notes: a — Assuming continuation of 1971–81 growth rates; b — Assuming continuation of 1971–81 growth rates

Source: Hughes (1985)

The 'poor white trash' image is merely the most extreme manifestation of a large literature focussing on differences in the growth of GDP between nations. The central message of this literature (or, at least, that section published in Australia) is that Australia has performed very badly while other countries have performed very well, and that the crucial objective of economic policy is to improve Australia's relative performance compared to our competitors. The way to do this, it is suggested, is to copy appropriately selected countries that have performed well. Popular examples have included Japan, Sweden, the United States of America (USA) and the countries of the Association of Southeast Asian Nations (ASEAN). Arguments of an analogous kind have been popular in many other countries, including most of those listed as exemplars for Australia.

Thus, much of the interest in the predictions of future (relative) poverty relates not to their accuracy as forecasts but to their rhetorical use in present-day policy debates. Australia's perceived decline is attributed to various aspects of our current socio-economic system, such as protection, regulation, taxation and industrial conflict, and we are urged to follow the example of our more successful neighbours, such as Japan and the ASEAN countries. Since these are a very diverse group, a wide range of policy positions can be supported in this way.

For example, in the 1983 election, the Australian Labor Party (ALP) used relative growth style arguments to support Bob Hawke's brand of corporatist consensus (which may be justified by a reference to Japanese examples). By contrast, most of the contributors to the AIPS study support free-market policies, Singapore and Hong Kong being the prime examples. With appropriate selections, a similar type of argument could be mounted for mercantilist or indicative-planning types of policy or, for that matter, for some form of 'guided democracy'.

This wide range of possibilities may suggest that the thesis is merely a debating point that can be used to stress the urgency of whatever policies the speaker favours. In fact, however, the adoption of relative GDP growth rates as a touchstone of policy success has significant and dangerous implications.

The objects of this article are twofold. The first is to show that the data used to back up the 'poor white trash' case can be highly misleading. In particular, Australia's apparent relative decline since 1870 has more to do with demographic factors than with mistaken economic policies. The second object is to argue that concern with relative economic growth rates as the major focus of economic policy is both mistaken and dangerous.

How much do relative living standards matter?

The first question to be asked is whether it would matter if the current trends in relative growth continued to the point where Australia's per capita income was below that of our South-East Asian neighbours. After all, the standard of living for most Australians is already fairly high, and the scenarios set out in typical projections of relative growth imply that they will continue to improve, although not as fast as those of other countries. Even in relative terms, our per capita income is only 5 to 10 per cent lower than that of most of the nations currently ahead of us and 20 per cent below that of the richest country in the world, the USA (this gap has narrowed significantly over the past 25 years). Thus, unless the South-East Asian nations ran far ahead of the entire world, our poor-nation status would be difficult to discern from a casual examination of living standards.

Most advocates of the 'poor white trash' thesis do not bother to address this issue, relying on the impact of its racist imagery and the general presumption that more is better. One writer who does address the issue is Helen Hughes (1985), who argues that there are two main reasons for concern.

The first is that 'young Australians will have to seek graduate studies or career opportunities in Tokyo or Singapore to be at the frontier of technological trends', while 'unskilled Australian workers will have to look for jobs as maids and waiters in Kuala Lumpur' (Hughes 1985). If this prospect is dismaying, it is worth noting that ambitious young Australians already go abroad (most of them to the USA) to be at the forefront of technological change and intellectual endeavour generally.

The apparent fear associated with the prospect of our South-East Asian neighbours taking over some of these roles would appear to carry with it a hint of racism. This tendency is obviously inherent in the 'poor white trash' terminology, and it is noteworthy that the AIPS deliberately avoided this phrase while carrying over many of the associated preconceptions.

A more serious threat, according to Hughes, is that our standing in the region, which depends on the fact that our economic weight is disproportionate to our small population, will be gradually eroded as our total GNP becomes smaller in relation to that of the region as a whole. But this is inevitable. There is no way that we can prevent the ASEAN nations from catching up to the developed world in general, and Australia in particular. The best that can be hoped for, in terms of relative economic performance, is that Australia's per capita GNP will remain somewhat higher than that of our neighbours. Even if this is achieved, our small population means that our absolute GNP cannot continue to be as large in relation to that of the region as a whole as it has been in the past.

It does not seem that the relative growth debate is very useful in adapting to these realities. Moreover, this argument concerns absolute GNP, while the relative growth debate is almost always couched in terms of per capita growth rates. As Table 1.1 shows, Australia's performance in terms of absolute GNP growth has been quite good. Over the period 1870–1976, only three developed nations managed higher rates of growth in absolute GDP than Australia. Performance over the postwar period was similarly reasonable according to this criterion.

An alternative ground for concern over low relative per capita GDP growth rates is that they are an indicator of poor economic management, or, more generally, of social institutions being antagonistic to growth. It is important to consider how useful an indication is provided by low relative GDP growth rates.

Some observations on relative growth rates

Before considering any international comparisons of economic performance, it is important to note that slightly different methods can yield massively different results. Castles (1986) shows that in terms of purchasing power for standard consumer commodity baskets, Australia is still in the top 10 countries of the OECD and has shown no perceptible slide. The same difficulties arise for countries other than Australia. Dowrick and Nguyen (1986), using the criterion of per capita GDP in 1975 in US dollars, show Switzerland as experiencing a relative decline, parallel to Australia. By contrast, Kasper (1986), using 1980 prices and exchange rates, shows Switzerland as leading the world throughout the postwar period.

Even sharper changes arise when an alternative criterion of assessment is applied. For example, differing comparisons have been made on the basis of levels, growth rates, and changes in growth rates of per capita GDP. In general, countries that do well on the first criterion (such as the USA) are likely to do badly on the second (the convergence effect examined by Dowrick and Nguyen), while those that do well on the second (such as Japan) are likely to do badly on the third.

There is no reason to confine attention to per capita GDP. Given the fairly small differences between the developed countries, it would seem reasonable to consider factors such as the labour–leisure trade-off and the equality of income distribution before making any comparison of prosperity or economic performance. Even a 10 per cent difference in working hours could offset a shift of about six places on Dowrick and Nguyen's league table.

For example, many workers in the USA work a 40-hour week, with two weeks of annual leave, no long service leave and about six public holidays per year, implying approximately 245 working days in the year. A comparable Australian with four weeks annual leave, a monthly rostered day off (associated with the 38-hour week), 11 or 12 public holidays and long service leave would work about 210 days per year, or about 15 per cent less. This is almost exactly enough to offset the difference in per capita GDP between the two countries. Similarly, as regards equality of income distribution, few would doubt that Sweden is a better country in which to be (comparatively) poor than the USA.

Indeed, an appropriate selection of time periods and criteria can make any nation look good or bad. For example, it is currently fashionable to compare the 'dynamic' US economy with the hidebound and over-regulated economies of western Europe. Yet, only a few years ago, the USA was being compared unfavourably to these very countries. All that has happened in the interim is that the USA has moved from a trough to a peak on the business cycle. Over the post-1973 period as a whole, the USA has done slightly worse than most European economies.

It is quite straightforward even to make a country like Japan look bad. For example, Norton and Mcdonald (1981) compare a number of countries on the basis of changes in rates of unemployment, inflation and growth since 1973. Their purpose is to compare Australia's performance with that of other countries, but when their criterion is applied to changes in growth rates, Japan is the worst performer in the OECD.

A crucial feature of the data listed in Tables 1.1–1.3 is the tendency for the less developed nations to catch up. This reflects, among other things, the fact that it is easier to copy or adapt existing technologies to make productivity improvements than it is to develop new technologies from scratch. This tendency is not universal; with sufficient mismanagement, a lagging country can fall even further behind. However, as Gruen (1982), and Dowrick and Nguyen (1986), have shown, there is a general tendency for growth rates to be higher for those nations that are initially worse off. Thus, during the period when she specialised in 'copycat' manufacturing, Japan recorded annual growth rates of the order of 10 per cent. When Japan became a technological leader in the 1970s, her growth rates fell to 3 or 4 per cent, and it was poorer South-East Asian nations that recorded strikingly rapid growth.

It is worth considering the extrapolations presented by Hughes in the light of this convergence effect. They are based on the assumption that the ASEAN nations can continue their current (or, rather, 1970–81) growth rates long after they have caught up to and surpassed Australia, and, for that matter, the other developed nations. Such an extrapolation implies that, by the year 2131, Singapore would have a per capita GDP nine times as large as that of the OECD nations but would still be growing more than twice as fast.

Dowrick and Nguyen (1986) cite a number of estimates showing that, all things being equal, a poor nation should catch up two-thirds of the difference with a rich one over a period of 25 years. As levels of GDP converge, so, in general, do rates of GDP growth. An important consequence of this 'catch-up' effect is the sharp decline in the variance of per capita GDP among the developed nations. Since 1973, differences in rates of growth have also fallen sharply.

The other major factor that has been shown to affect the rate of growth of per capita GDP is population growth. In general, studies of comparative growth indicate that a 1 per cent increase in the rate of population growth is associated with an increase in total GDP of between 0.3 and 0.9 per cent. Since this is less than the increase in population growth, per capita GDP growth is reduced as population growth increases.

One noteworthy issue that can only be mentioned briefly is the relationship between economic growth and spending on armaments. In the classical theory of economic growth, armaments expenditure is a straightforward subtraction from savings devoted to productive investment. On the other hand, there has been an influential school of thought suggesting that 'military Keynesianism' has played a vital role in preventing stagnation and promoting growth.

Looking at the best and worst performers in Table 1.2, the United Kingdom and Japan, it is noteworthy that one has struggled to maintain Imperial pretensions, while the other has been forcibly prevented from making major arms expenditures. Of all possible paths to greater worldwide prosperity, a reduction in arms spending seems both the most appealing and one of the most practical.

In general, however, the most important point to be derived from the study of international growth rates is the fact that differences in both total levels of GDP and the rate of growth of GDP have become generally smaller over the postwar period. Differences in growth rates among the developed nations since 1973 have been very small indeed, with 15 of the 24 nations, including Australia, falling in a range of only 1.5 per cent. As regards the developed nations, relative growth is an issue whose time has passed.

Assessing Australia's performance

1870–1930

In light of these general comments on international comparisons, what can be said about Australia's economic performance? Perhaps the most important feature of Table 1.1 is that the period of sharpest decline is the 60 years from 1870 to 1930. Since 1930, Australia's per capita GDP has moved broadly in line with that of other developed countries, although it has been slightly below average. Several observations may be made at this point.

First, there is not much value in scrutinising our present institutions for the sources of poor economic performance in a period before many of these institutions were formed. For example, many commentators place a great deal of stress on highly protected industries such as motor vehicles and textiles. Yet the motor vehicle industry only dates from the Second World War, while the first tariffs on textiles were imposed in 1926. If comparisons of relative growth are to be the touchstone of economic performance, it would seem that the high protection of these activities has greatly improved our performance. Even such a venerable body as tthe Arbitration Commission (previously the Arbitration Court) only dates from 1904, towards the end of the period of sharpest decline.

Second, while Australia's comparatively poor performance since 1870 is blamed on various defects in our sociopolitical system and, particularly, on government policies, no corresponding analysis is given to the previous century. During this period, European Australia was transformed from a starving convict settlement imposed on a continent occupied by hunter–

gatherers[3] to the richest society (in terms of measured per capita GDP) the world had ever seen. It is rarely suggested that this spectacularly good performance was the result of brilliant management by the rulers of the time. Rather, it is attributed to luck in the form of our endowments of natural resources. For many writers it is this endowment of natural resources that makes our decline in relative growth rates since 1870 so difficult to believe. This betrays muddled thinking. The price of primary commodities relative to other goods has fallen significantly over the last century so our endowment of natural resources is much less of an advantage now than it was in 1870. Therefore, contrary to the popular view, it would have been surprising if Australia (or any other primary commodity exporter) had maintained higher than average rates of growth over this period.

The discussion so far has implicitly incorporated the assumption that measured GDP per capita is a useful basis for comparison. However, some features of the Australian data make it particularly unreliable for this purpose. First, the data presented by Hughes are based on population counts that exclude Aboriginal people,[4] although their (low-paid or unpaid) labour made a significant contribution to measured GDP. Since Aboriginal people formed 9 per cent of the population in 1870 and only about 1 per cent in 1930, both the initial level of per capita GDP and the subsequent decline are exaggerated to this extent.

Second, the European population in 1870 was very atypical, reflecting a frontier society with high rates of immigration (predominantly by young adult males) and a small initial population. In particular, the masculinity ratio (the ratio of males to females) was much higher than for other developed countries. Furthermore, this ratio was highest in the most productive age group (those between 15 and 65). Since measured GDP is dominated by the work of men and excludes much of the work done by women, it is not surprising that Australia's measured GDP per capita should be very high. Over the period 1870–1930, Australia's masculinity ratio approached that of the USA (Table 1.4). The Australian population was also significantly younger on average than that of other nations. For example, in 1870 the

---

3   Since this article was published, scholarly and public discussion of Aboriginal land management has emphasised the role of active practices, including forms of agriculture and aquaculture and the use of fire to manage landscapes (Gammage 2012; Reeder-Myers, L, Braje, TJ, Hofman, CA, et al. 2022). Nevertheless, monetary measures such as GDP, the central topic of this chapter, are not applicable to Aboriginal society before European contact. GDP measures are only meaningful in the context of a market economy.

4   The term 'Aboriginal' also encompassed Torres Strait Islanders.

proportion of Australians aged over 65 was only 1.7 per cent compared with 3.6 per cent for the USA and 7 per cent for the UK. While this was offset by a correspondingly higher number of children, the workforce overall was substantially younger than that of other countries. In an era when capacity for hard physical work was essential, this was conducive to high per capita GDP. Once again, Australia approached the international norm in this respect over the period 1870–1930, and this was reflected in a decline in relative per capita GDP.

Table 1.4 Masculinity ratios 1870–1930

	AUSTRALIA	UK	USA
1870	121	95	102
1880	117	95	104
1890	116	94	105
1900	110	94	104
1910	108	91	106
1920	103	92	104
1930	103	92	102

Sources: US Bureau of the Census — Vital statistics: Rates (various years); UK General Register Office Census Reports (various); 'Population of Australia'; *ESCAP Country Monograph* 9

Australia now appears not as an extreme outlier but as a member of a group of leading nations, including the UK and the Low Countries. While it is apparent that the USA overtook this group between 1870 and 1930, and that several other countries have caught up, the picture of dramatic relative decline derived from GDP per capita may be seen to be greatly exaggerated.

1930 to the present

Although the data presented in Table 1.1 have been shown to be misleading, there is no doubt that Australia's economic performance before about 1930 was somewhat unusual. For most policy purposes, however, it is more useful to consider the subsequent period, and in particular the period since the end of the Second World War. During this period, Australia's per capita GDP growth performance was anything but unusual. As Table 1.2 shows, it was within 0.5 per cent of the average for the 12 richest nations in each of the three sub-periods.

Dowrick and Nguyen (1986) provide a more formal test of performance. They estimate several equations that relate per capita GDP growth in a range of countries to initial income levels and population growth rates. Australia's growth rate is almost exactly that predicted by the equations, with the deviation ranging from +0.5 per cent to –0.3 per cent. Similar results are obtained by Gruen (1986), using a slightly different dataset.

How can this be squared with the dire statistics of our slip down the international ladder presented by advocates of the white trash thesis? As we have seen, convergence means that differences between income levels should shrink. Thus, it is not surprising that Australia's per capita GDP has grown more slowly than that of nations that were initially poorer.

However, this alone cannot account for the fact that some nations have overtaken us. The explanation offered by the international growth models is that Australia's population has been growing about 1 per cent faster than the OECD average. This implies a reduction in relative per capita GDP growth of about 0.4 per cent. Because differences in income levels among developed countries are now very small, even such a small difference implies a large slip down a ladder of comparative levels. In essence, this says more about the pointlessness of such league tables than anything else.

A point of particular relevance in the assessment of Australia's economic performance is that, until recently, Australian policy has focussed on absolute as much as per capita GDP. This has reflected defence concerns and the existence of a generally shared ideology of development. Thus, while it may be suggested that immigration and tariff policies have led to a lower per capita GDP than might otherwise have been possible, it should be recognised that these policies were implemented with a general acceptance that some constraints in average income were a reasonable price to pay for more rapid absolute growth.

This acceptance is quite explicit, for example, in the Brigden Report, and is implicit in the rejection of standard economic criteria for the assessment of projects seen as promoting 'development', notably through irrigation and Northern development. Current views, including my own, tend to place a low or even negative value on development and population growth per se. In assessing past performance, however, we should be clear that our predecessors did not miss the target. Rather, they aimed at, and hit, a different target.

One aspect of the relative growth debate and the current economic crisis has been a series of conflicting claims on the role of migration. Geoffrey Blainey and others have called for restrictions on migration as a response to recession, while Helen Hughes and others have proposed a return to the mass immigration policies of the 1950s and 1960s as a response to poor relative performance. The debate has been confusing and, frequently, confused.

One major source of confusion has been a failure to distinguish between short-term macro-economic effects of migration and longer-term effects on growth in per capita incomes. Oddly enough, the evidence here suggests that both sides have got their arguments back to front. The critics of immigration have generally focussed on short-term employment effects, but the evidence here suggests that these are neutral or slightly favourable.

On the other hand, advocates of mass immigration have frequently focussed on long-term effects, but the evidence, including that provided by Gruen, and Dowrick and Nguyen, supports the view that high population growth tends to reduce per capita GDP growth. It is likely that the effects of migration will be somewhat more favourable than those of high rates of natural increase, since migrants are likely to be people of working age. Nevertheless, the evidence does not support the proposition that mass immigration is likely to promote high rates of growth in per capita (as opposed to total) GDP.

Both sides of the debate share the view that migration policy should be determined primarily by fairly narrow economic considerations. This is a natural consequence of the 'relative growth' approach. In my view, policy should primarily reflect social decisions on the costs and benefits of greater cultural diversity, higher population densities and other such effects of expanded migration. We should view with suspicion any claim that our economic circumstances necessitate either sharp reductions or massive increases in immigration.

Playing the relative growth game

In the preceding sections, the specific contentions made by the 'poor white trash' school have been criticised. The object of this section is to examine the general implications of this mode of argument. The misleading claims made by users of these arguments reflect the biases inherent in their manner of assessing economic performance.

One noteworthy feature is a strong tendency to select and present statistics in such a way as to make relative economic performance for any particular country look bad. Conversely, it is possible to select statistics that make any particular country look good, and this exercise is occasionally undertaken by governments facing re-election. However, in most countries, the purpose of international comparisons is typically to demonstrate the poor relative performance of the country concerned, and hence to emphasise the urgency of adopting whatever policies the person making the comparison wishes to advocate. Viewed simply as a way of emphasising the urgency of one's case, the relative growth game may seem harmless enough. In fact, however, it yields a seriously distorted attitude to economic policy issues.

For example, it would be generally agreed that Australia's economic performance since 1973 has been considerably worse than during the postwar period from 1945 to 1973. However, a concern with relative growth rates yields precisely the opposite conclusion. During the relevant period, Australia's per capita growth rate has been much closer to the OECD average than in earlier periods.

A second feature of this approach is that it focusses attention on narrow measures of GNP without any concern for quality of life. In a general context, even the most rigidly orthodox economist would recognise that increases in GNP are not necessarily beneficial if they are obtained at the expense of increased working hours. In mainstream economic theory, what matters is that the allocation of resources should reflect individual preferences regarding the relative value of increased leisure and higher income.

Distortions arise when outcomes diverge from these preferences. Yet, in the context of the relative efficiency debate, Hughes feels free to write that in Australia, 'a high preference for leisure distorts the allocation of resources'. Calls for increased working hours, shorter holidays and other improved conditions have been common. Less tangible aspects of the quality of life, such as the protection of the environment, are typically ignored completely in this debate, except as sources of needless regulation.

The distribution of income is another issue that goes by the board in this approach. Indeed, players of the relative growth game such as Michael Porter are concerned to decry disputes over the distribution of income as a major obstacle to the good of 'the community as a whole', which is typically measured by average per capita income. In the context of very poor developing countries, one could perhaps argue that an increase in the size of the cake matters more than more equitable sharing, since the achievement of an average income comparable to that of the developed world would make almost everyone better off.

It is, however, very difficult to apply this argument to the developed world. The wellbeing of the poor in a range of developed countries is largely independent of the minor variations between them in average income. For example, the USA has a per capita income 20 per cent larger than that of the other developed countries, but its performance on measures such as infant mortality and homelessness, which are closely related to levels of deprivation, are among the worst in the developed world.

A more subtle feature of the relative growth game is the way in which key policy issues are prejudged. For example, there is considerable scope for debate over the importance of external competitiveness as compared to measures of domestic wellbeing such as unemployment levels. The relative growth approach implies a single-minded concern with competitiveness on the assumption that everything else will come right in the end. This is seen at its worst in the prolonged deflation imposed by Margaret Thatcher, which, after her serving two terms in office, has yet to produce tangible domestic benefits.

A second important feature of the relative growth game is that issues relating to the overall world economy are largely ignored. This is despite the fact that, among the developed countries, the worst performers prior to 1973 did almost as well as the best performers since 1973. Insofar as the sharp downturn since 1973 is discussed at all in the relative growth literature, it is typically regarded either as the result of an exogenous shock in the form of the increase in Organization of the Petroleum Exporting Countries (OPEC) oil prices or as the result of mistaken domestic policies adopted independently (but simultaneously) by a large number of different countries.

The most important topic of economic analysis should attempt to analyse the problems of the world economy and seek to propose remedies at a global level. The relative growth approach totally excludes this task from the agenda. Severe difficulties, particularly in the form of intractable trade deficits, have been encountered by countries that have attempted to maintain growth rates substantially in excess of those of their trading partners. Examples include countries as diverse in their institutional structure and policy background as France, Australia and the USA.

Against this backdrop, supporters of the relative growth approach point to the success of the East Asian countries in maintaining high growth rates. In the last two years, however, the Philippines has entered a seemingly intractable economic crisis, South Korea has encountered significant balance-of-payments problems, and Singapore has issued forecasts of negative real growth. All of these problems may be traced to low export demand associated with the poor performance of the world economy as a whole. Players of the relative growth game have essentially nothing to say about this issue.

Concluding comments

Prophets of all kinds have long found predictions of impending doom an indispensable aid in gaining and holding the attention of their audiences, especially when they can promise that careful obedience to the prophet's commands is the only method of averting this doom. The prediction that Australians will soon be the poor white trash of Asia has been used in precisely this fashion.

While shock tactics may sometimes be salutary, it is extremely unfortunate that the advocates of this approach have chosen to focus on minor, and rapidly decreasing, differences in growth rates at a time when growth throughout the developed world has been painfully slow. The prospect of significant worldwide falls in rates of growth, and even in the actual level of per capita income, is uncomfortably close. In this light, arguments about which nation is doing the least badly are not merely irrelevant but positively damaging to prospects for international cooperation.

There is, no doubt, substantial scope for improvement in Australian economic performance within the constraints imposed by the world economy. Efforts towards such an improvement are likely to be more rewarding if they are motivated by the desire to improve the lives of Australians rather than a need to keep up with the international Joneses.

Bibliography

Castles, Ian. 1986. 'Is Australia's Slide Down the "League Table" a Myth?'. Paper presented at the Centre for Economic Policy Research, The Australian National University, Conference on Recent Australian Economic Growth, November 1986.

Dowrick, Steve and Duc-Tho Nguyen. 1986. 'Australia's Post-war Economic Growth: Measurement and International Comparison'. Paper presented at the Centre for Economic Policy Research, The Australian National University, Conference on Recent Australian Economic Growth. November 1986.

Gammage, B. 2012. *The Biggest Estate on Earth: How Aborigines Made Australia.* Sydney: Allen & Unwin.

Gruen, Fred. 1982. 'How Bad Is Australia's Economic Performance and Why?'. *Economic Record* 62: 180–93. doi.org/10.1111/j.1475-4932.1986.tb00893.x.

Hughes, Helen. 1985. 'Australia and the World Environment: The Dynamics of International Competition and Wealth Creation'. In *Poor Nation of the Pacific?: Australia's Future?*, edited by Jocelynne E. Scutt, 1–17. Sydney: Allen & Unwin.

Kasper, Wolfgang. 1986. 'Structural Change for Economic Growth'. *Economic Affairs* 6, no. 5 (June–July): 8–13. doi.org/10.1111/j.1468-0270.1986.tb01773.x.

Norton, WE and Robin McDonald. 1981. 'Implications for Australia of Cross-Country Comparisons of Economic Performance'. *Economic Record* 57, no. 159: 301–18. doi.org/10.1111/j.1475-4932.1981.tb01067.x.

Porter, M. 1985. 'The Labour of Liberalisation'. In *Poor Nation of the Pacific?: Australia's Future?*, edited by Jocelynne E. Scutt, 37–61. Sydney: Allen & Unwin.

Quiggin, John. 1987. 'White Trash of Asia'. *Current Affairs Bulletin* 64: 18–25.

Reeder-Myers, Leslie, Todd J. Braje, Courney A. Hofman, Emma A. Elliott Smith, Carey J. Garland, Michael Grone, Carla S. Hadden, et al. 2022. Indigenous oyster fisheries persisted for millennia and should inform future management. *Nature Communications* 13, Article no. 2383. doi.org/10.1038/s41467-022-29818-z.

Scutt, Jocelynne E., ed. 1985. *Poor Nation of the Pacific?: Australia's Future?* Sydney: Allen & Unwin.

2

The evolution of neoliberalism

Most recently published in 2022 as Quiggin, John. 'The Evolution of Neoliberalism'. In *Sustainability and the New Economics,* edited by Stephen Williams and Rod Taylor. Cham, Switzerland: Springer. doi.org/10.1007/ 978-3-030-78795-0_6.

An earlier version was published as Quiggin, John. 2018. 'Neoliberalism: Rise, Decline and Future Prospects'. In *The SAGE Handbook of Neoliberalism,* edited by Damien Cahill, Chapter 11.

Introduction

The term 'neoliberalism' is widely used, and it is often misused and misunderstood. Properly understood, it is the ideological underpinning of the era of financialised capitalism that emerged from the economic crises of the early 1970s and remained dominant for the rest of the 20th century. Its central idea was that markets, particularly financial markets, generally outperform governments in the allocation of resources and investments. Neoliberalism came in a variety of forms, reflecting the variety of liberalism itself, but it was different from preceding forms of liberalism because of the need to respond to the successes and failures of social democracy in the second half of the 20th century. In one form or another, neoliberalism became the unquestioned basis for the thinking of both centre-right and centre-left parties around the world.[1]

---

1   Ideology always looks like common sense from the inside. That is why supporters of neoliberalism hardly ever use this term (or any ideological term) to describe themselves, and why they are so hostile to being labelled in this way.

The era of unquestioned neoliberal dominance came to a sudden end on 15 September 2008, when the bank and financial services firm Lehmann Brothers filed for bankruptcy. This collapse signalled the failure of attempts by the US authorities to manage the crisis that had originated in markets for housing loans to 'subprime' (that is, low-income or high-risk) borrowers. Within a week, the global financial system was in crisis, and governments were forced to engage in massive bailouts.

The years since the Global Financial Crisis (GFC) have been characterised by chronic upheaval. The bailouts needed to prevent the collapse of the financial system in turn produced fiscal crises, most notably the sovereign debt crisis in the European Union (EU). These crises were resolved by austerity policies that produced drastic cuts in public services and living standards while leaving the financial sector essentially unscathed. As a result of the crises, the neoliberal consensus that had prevailed up to the GFC broke down. On the political left, radical critics of capitalism such as Jeremy Corbyn and Bernie Sanders challenged the 'Third Way' doctrines of Tony Blair and Bill Clinton. On the political right, the loss of faith in neoliberalism was reflected in the British withdrawal from the EU, known as Brexit, and the election of Donald Trump to the presidency of the USA.

The final shock came with the COVID-19 pandemic. Faced with a drastic economic upheaval, governments around the world responded with intervention on a massive scale. Dogmas about balanced budgets and the perils of public debt, already honoured more in the breach than the observance, were discarded overnight. The pandemic required massive intervention in labour markets, housing, financial markets, the health system and international trade. Some of these interventions will be unwound when the pandemic recedes, but not all. The system that emerges from the pandemic will undoubtedly be capitalist and more or less inequitable, but it will not, in any meaningful sense, be neoliberal.

The aim of this chapter is to describe the evolution of neoliberalism, beginning as an oppositional movement in the era of Keynesian social democracy and the Bretton Woods system, attaining dominance from the early 1970s onwards and collapsing in the face of the crises of the 21st century. Prospects for the future will be considered briefly.

The chapter is organised as follows. Section 1 presents neoliberalism in relation to liberalism, the intellectual tradition from which social liberalism and social democracy are also primarily derived. A distinction is drawn between 'hard' and 'soft' versions of neoliberalism. Section 2 describes the rise of social democracy, focussing particularly on the period following the Great Depression, which largely discredited the classical liberal model on which neoliberalism is based. The crisis of the 1970s, and the failure of social democracy to present an adequate response, are the focus of Section 3. Section 4 is devoted to the rise of neoliberalism, both as an ideology, and as a political and economic force gaining its strength from the massive expansion of the financial sector. After that, in Section 5, we focus specifically on soft neoliberalism, the modified version of neoliberalism adopted by social democratic parties in the 1980s and 1990s. Section 6 deals with the decline of neoliberalism, from the crises of the late 1990s to the GFC of 2008. In Section 7 we examine the political implications of the failure of neoliberalism. A three-party model is presented, in which the main movements driving contemporary politics are categorised as neoliberal (soft or hard), tribalist and leftist. In conclusion, we discuss the requirements for a successful left response to the crisis and offer some suggestions for a way forward.

What is neoliberalism?

The evolution of neoliberalism has been a complex process, exacerbated by disputes over the meaning, and even the legitimacy, of the term. It is widely seen as a meaningless, all-purpose pejorative.

The need for a definition of an ideological movement is felt much more by its critics than by its supporters. Ideology always looks like common sense from the inside, and a dominant ideology just seems like 'what everyone knows'. For this reason, followers of a dominant ideology resist the use of any specific name or label to describe their position.

One result is that labels of this kind, including 'neoliberalism', are almost always used negatively and, as a result, overused to refer to anything the speaker dislikes. In a discussion of broader historical and political trends, however, 'neoliberalism' is too useful a term to forego, despite the confusion that surrounds it. Instead, we need to address some of the sources of this confusion.

As the name implies, neoliberalism is a descendant of liberalism, a tradition that, in various forms, underlies most contemporary streams of political thought. An obvious starting point is the greatest of 19th-century liberals,

John Stuart Mill. Mill is best known today for his strong defence of free speech, his advocacy for equality for women and his steadfast opposition to slavery. Over the course of his lifetime, his views on economic issues shifted from the free-market orthodoxy of classical economics to an abstract form of socialism.

All these aspects of Mill's thought are reflected in different streams of liberal thought. From Mill onwards in North America and most of the English-speaking world, the dominant version of liberalism was social liberalism, combining support for civil liberties with advocacy for a range of government policies to limit income inequality and alleviate poverty.

In Europe, from the early 20th century onwards, social liberalism was largely subsumed by social democratic and labour movements. The term 'liberal' was more closely associated with the political right, and with free-market economic analysis, in which Millian concerns about free speech were less prominent. This tendency is sometimes referred to as 'classical liberalism'.

The term neoliberalism embodies these ambiguities and has been coined at least twice to apply to different, but closely related, developments within liberalism. I will distinguish these as soft and hard neoliberalism.

In the USA, the term neoliberalism was used from the 1990s onwards to describe a shift to the right by social liberals, particularly those termed 'New Democrats'.[2] Here, the key ideas were a focus on 'sound' economic management, acceptance of financial deregulation and market-based policies more generally, and avoidance of class rhetoric.

In one form or another, soft versions of neoliberalism came to dominate social liberal and social democratic parties throughout the English-speaking world. The term 'Third Way' was often applied to this development (Giddens 1998; Giddens 2000), with the suggestion that this approach represented a new development in social democracy rather than a capitulation to its opponents.

In the European context, the term neoliberalism (and the closely related idea of 'ordoliberalism') was first used as early as 1938 to describe attempts to develop an updated version of classical liberalism capable of responding

---

2   'New Labour' in the UK was part of the same 'Third Way' movement. A cynic might observe, with reference to products like 'New Coke', that the attachment of the term 'New' to an existing movement is rarely a good sign.

to the crisis created by the Great Depression and, after 1945, of competing with the social democratic welfare state (Hartwich 2009). The result was a 'hard' form of neoliberalism in which concessions to social democratic ideas were limited as far as possible. In the US context, where the term neoliberalism referred to the soft variety, hard neoliberalism was most commonly described as 'free market conservatism' (Nell 1984).

Because it was based primarily on a critique of social democracy, hard neoliberalism placed more weight on economic freedom than personal freedom or civil liberties, reversing the emphasis of classical liberalism. On matters of personal freedom, hard neoliberalism is basically agnostic, encompassing a range of views from repressive traditionalism to libertarianism.

In terms of economic policy, neoliberalism is constrained by the need to compete with the achievements of social democracy. Hence, it was inconsistent with the kind of dogmatic libertarianism that would leave the poor to starvation or private charity and education to parents.

The need to compete with the appeal of social democracy has continued in the period of neoliberal dominance. As a result, the importance of the public sector—as measured, for example, by the revenue share of national income—has remained largely unchanged despite extensive efforts towards privatisation and deregulation.

The rise of neoliberalism in the 1970s

In the decades after 1945, social democratic ideas were dominant throughout the developed world. Whether or not social democratic parties held office, they drove the policy debate, to the extent that terms like 'progressive' inherently incorporated the notion of 'progress in the direction of more social democracy' (Quiggin 2003).

The starting point of 20th-century social democracy was the combination of the welfare state, macro-economic stabilisation and the mixed economy. Their combined effect was to transform the lived experience of capitalist society.

The risks of falling into destitution as a result of unemployment, illness or old age, previously an ever-present reality for the great majority of workers, were eliminated almost completely by social security systems and, except in the USA, publicly provided health care. However, the trends that would produce the neoliberal counterrevolution were already evident.

The last years of the social democratic era saw a struggle over income distribution that virtually guaranteed an inflationary outburst. Union militancy, fuelled in many countries by Marxist rhetoric, came into sharp conflict with an emerging speculative capitalism, driven by revived global financial markets. Firms raised prices to meet wage demands, spurring yet further wage demands to compensate for higher prices and maintain living standards (Brenner et al. 2010).

Previous episodes of inflation had been brought under control quite rapidly through Keynesian contractionary policies. Unfortunately, these policies were becoming less effective as inflationary expectations became embedded and as the social restraint generated by memories of the Depression broke down.

The critical event was the breakdown, in the opening years of the 1970s, of the Bretton Woods system of fixed exchange rates that had been the basis of the international financial system within which Keynesian macro-economics operated. The *coup de grace* came with the oil shock of 1973, which was both a reflection of the inflationary outburst that was already under way and the cause of a further upsurge.

Within a couple of years, the entire edifice of postwar prosperity had collapsed, and the Keynesian 'Golden Age' came to a painful and chaotic end. Meanwhile, the collapse of the Bretton Woods system led to a self-perpetuating cycle in which the rapid growth of international financial flows led to the breakdown of both domestic and international financial regulations, allowing yet further expansion of the financial sector.

In the decades following the breakdown of the Bretton Woods system, financial sector activity exploded and was almost completely decoupled from any connection to real economic activity. By 2014, global financial market transactions totalled $US4 trillion each day, or more than 20 times real economic activity. Trade in derivatives was even larger, with notional outstanding volumes of at least US$500 trillion (Bank for International Settlements 2015).

With this growth in activity came hugely increased power and profitability. As early as 1987, financial firms were being described as the 'Masters of the Universe', a phrase coined in Tom Wolfe's (1987) novel, *The Bonfire of the Vanities*. The rise of the financial sector, and the concomitant decline of the trade union movement, tipped the balance of political power in favour of neoliberalism.

Hard neoliberalism

Although the rising political power of the financial markets facilitated the general shift towards neoliberalism, this development also depended on a resurgence of neoliberal policy ideas. In sharp contrast with social democrats, the advocates of neoliberalism were ready with answers to the crisis of the 1970s.

In macro-economics, the monetarist critique of Keynesianism developed by Friedman (1968) was rapidly accepted, eventually evolving into the inflation-targeting regime that remained in effect until the GFC.

In fiscal policy, the 'tax revolts' of the 1970s led to a consensus on the need to restrain the growth of government. The perceived success of airline deregulation in the USA led to a broader movement in favour of deregulation and privatisation. To emphasise the distinction from macro-economic policy, these policies were frequently referred to as 'micro-economic reform' (Quiggin 1996). This phrase captured the positive connotations of 'reform', a term long used to describe liberal and social democratic policy innovations while reversing the substantive content.

The advocacy of Friedman (1962), and Friedman and Friedman (1980), played a crucial role in promoting free market conservatism in the USA. Many of these ideas had been developed by economists associated with the University of Chicago, where Friedman worked for most of his long career.

In the UK, a crucial role was played by 'think tanks' such as the Institute of Economic Affairs (Cockett 1995).[3] The ideas developed by these think tanks formed the basis for the first systematic implementation of a neoliberal policy program, undertaken by the government of Margaret Thatcher in the UK from 1979 onwards.

---

3   The same was true in Australia (Cahill and Beder 2005).

The core goals of the program were to:

1. abandon Keynesian macro-economic stabilisation, based on active fiscal policy, in favour of an independent central bank with a directive to control inflation at all costs
2. remove the state altogether from 'non-core' functions through privatisation of government business enterprises and the sale of public housing
3. reject redistribution of income except for a basic 'safety net'
4. minimise the role of the state in core functions such as health, education and income security through contracting out, voucher schemes and so on.

Thatcher attained the first and second of these goals very successfully. Although policies of monetary contraction implemented in 1979 produced a deep recession, with millions left unemployed, the government persisted and succeeded in bringing an end to the inflationary upsurge of the 1970s. Most of the publicly owned infrastructure sector (electricity, water, telecommunications, airports and railways) was privatised.

The UK government made considerably less progress on the third and fourth objectives. There were also substantial reductions in the progressivity of the tax system, but Thatcher's most ambitious move in this direction, the replacement of council rates with a poll tax, was a disaster, leading, eventually, to her downfall. The attempt to wind back public involvement in health and education was similarly limited, meeting particular resistance in the case of the National Health Service. The result was that, although the scope of public sector activity was wound back through privatisation, the size of government was not. The century-old trend of growth in the share of national income going to the government was halted in the 1970s but not reversed.

Thatcher's ideas formed the core of a hard neoliberalism that rapidly became dominant throughout the English-speaking world. It was embodied in such documents as the *Fightback!* plan put forward by the Liberal and National parties in Australia in 1993 and the Contract with America proposed by the US Republican Party led by Newt Gingrich in 1994. Although neither of these programs produced immediate electoral success, most of the policies they proposed were eventually implemented.

Beyond the English-speaking world, the global spread of neoliberalism was driven less by political advocacy and more by international institutions. The debt crises of the 1990s produced what Williamson (1990) described as the Washington Consensus, a term that reflected the shared views of the US Treasury, the International Monetary Fund (IMF) and the World Bank, all based in Washington DC.

Less remarked upon, but equally significant, was the Europe-based consensus of the OECD, the European Commission and the European Central Bank (ECB). The ECB, created in the 1990s as part of the political project of unifying Europe around a common currency, represents a particularly pure institutional embodiment of hard neoliberalism (Palley 2013).

The rise of neoliberal ideas reinforced, and was reinforced by, the resurgence of faith in the financial sector. During the ascendancy of social democracy, banking had been boring, safe and tightly regulated. The emblems of capitalism in the mixed economy were industrial firms like General Motors and General Electric.[4] By contrast, the breakdown of social democracy in the 1970s saw the rise of financialised capitalism, dominated by global banks like Citibank, and Wall Street investment banks such as Goldman Sachs.

The key idea here was the efficient (financial) markets hypothesis. In its strong form, put forward by Fama (1970), the hypothesis states that financial markets provide the best possible estimate of the value of any investment. Although there was never any good supporting evidence for this claim, it became part of the 'common sense' of the neoliberal era. One result was the trepidation with which governments awaited the verdict of 'the markets' on budgets and other policy decisions.

Soft neoliberalism

The resurgence of a financialised form of global capitalism from the 1970s onwards came as a shock to the left. There were some attempts at resistance, notably by the Mitterand government, which came to office in France in 1980, but all such attempts failed in the face of the power of global capital markets. By the 1990s, the triumphalist decade that followed the collapse of

---

4   By the early 2000s, General Motors was a shadow of its former self, while General Electric had become, in essence, a finance company, dominated by its GE Capital business.

the Soviet Union, the dominance of neoliberalism was clearly re-established. Over the course of the 1980s and 1990s, most social democratic parties accommodated to the new realities.

As noted above, this accommodation was often presented as a new Third Way, allegedly transcending the dispute between social democrats and hard neoliberals. In reality, however, the Third Way amounted to little more than a soft version of neoliberalism (Callinicos 2001). Soft neoliberalism involved acceptance of most of the core elements of the neoliberal program, including privatisation, attacks on trade unions, uncritical acceptance of the dominant role of the financial sector, and attempts to halt or reverse the growth of the public sector.

Over the course of the 1980s and 1990s, most social democratic and liberal parties in the English-speaking world adopted soft neoliberalism in one form or another. Some examples, significant in themselves, but also symbolic of the shift in economic thinking include:

- the decision by the Hawke–Keating government in 1983 and 1985 to float the Australian dollar and deregulate the financial system
- the Clinton Administration's support for 'the end of welfare as we know it', demanded by the Gingrich-led Republican party in 1994. This measure was initially seen as successful because its adverse effects were masked by the strong growth of the 1990s. After growth slowed in the 2000s, however, the absence of welfare support contributed substantially to the growth of poverty. Even more striking were increasing mortality rates among significant groups, such as middle-aged white Americans
- Tony Blair's creation of a 'New Labour' party, in which the socialist objective formerly stated in Clause IV of its Constitution was abandoned (Labourcounts 2023). Before the change, the objective was stated as:

  [t]o secure for the workers by hand or by brain the full fruits of their industry and the most equitable distribution thereof that may be possible upon the basis of the common ownership of the means of production, distribution, and exchange, and the best obtainable system of popular administration and control of each industry or service.

- This changed to:

  a dynamic economy, serving the public interest, in which the enterprise of the market and the rigour of competition are joined with the forces of partnership and co-operation to produce the wealth the nation needs and the opportunity for all to work and prosper, with a thriving public sector and high quality services, where those undertakings essential to the common good are either owned by the public or accountable to them.

The rejection of public ownership embodied in the New Labour platform was reflected in policies of privatisation and private ownership of public infrastructure. Along with faith in the efficiency of financial markets, and acquiescence in, or support of, anti-union policies, support for privatisation represented one of the most consistent areas of agreement between soft and hard neoliberals. This support persisted, despite outcomes that ranged from mediocre to disastrous. The Private Finance Initiative, pursued with vigour by the Blair government in the UK, was one of the most notable examples of failure.

Despite accepting the core elements of hard neoliberalism, soft neoliberals attempted, in various ways, to mitigate the growing inequality that inevitably resulted from the implementation of the neoliberal program. In particular, soft neoliberal governments attempted to improve the functioning of the social welfare system rather than eliminating it or stripping it down to a minimal safety net. Nevertheless, the egalitarianism of traditional social democracy was abandoned, with arguments about the distribution of income and access to community services being replaced by discussion of safety nets or the efficient provision of services to 'customers'.

This shift was frequently expressed in terms of older debates about equality of opportunity as opposed to equality of outcomes. However, although the advocates of soft neoliberalism are particularly friendly to the upwardly mobile, the hostility to inherited privilege that characterised earlier advocates of equality of opportunity largely disappeared. Some supporters of soft neoliberalism took the argument to its logical conclusion, rejecting even the idea of equality of opportunity (Cavanagh 2003). This is at least consistent. In the presence of serious inequality of outcomes, it is impossible to prevent parents from passing their advantages on to their children. Under these circumstances, it is therefore impossible to achieve equality of opportunity.

More marked divisions arose in relation to social issues, particularly those related to multiculturalism, feminism and environmentalism. In the USA and Australia, the sharpness of these divisions, commonly referred to as 'culture wars', masked a substantial convergence on economic policy (Frank 2007).

The most successful implementation of soft neoliberalism was probably that of the Hawke–Keating Labor government in Australia between 1983 and 1996. The platform on which Labor was elected was an interventionist one, centred on the idea of an 'accord' on prices and wages. The Accord was negotiated between the Labor Party and the Australian Council of Trade Unions, of which Hawke had been a successful president, although it was hoped that a bargained consensus incorporating business groups could be achieved (Gruen and Grattan 1993).

The combination of financial market pressure and the spread of neoliberal ideas ensured that the government took a different direction, beginning with the decisions, in 1983 and 1984, to float the dollar and undertake substantial deregulation of the financial system. However, the success of the Accord in constraining wage growth and allowing a non-inflationary recovery from the recession of the early 1980s was an important countervailing force. Another example was the failure of the hard neoliberal reform of the tax system favoured by the then treasurer Paul Keating, based on the idea of using a goods and services tax (GST) to finance cuts in the top marginal rate of income tax. In the face of resistance from the union movement, and a lack of support from business, Prime Minister Bob Hawke rejected Keating's preferred option. Instead, the government implemented a reform program with substantial progressive elements such as a capital gains tax. The Hawke–Keating government also redesigned the social welfare system, integrating it with the tax system and maintaining or improving its progressive redistributive effects (Gruen and Grattan 1993).

The relative success of soft neoliberalism under Hawke and Keating was not sufficient to prevent growth in inequality over time, or the development of a bloated and dangerously unstable financial system. Nevertheless, a measure of their success can be gained by looking at the disastrous performance of New Zealand, where both the Labour government elected in 1983 and the National Party government that succeeded it from 1990 to 1999 embraced hard neoliberalism in a particularly doctrinaire form and with substantially worse economic outcomes (Hazledine and Quiggin 2006).

Thus, the differences between hard and soft neoliberalism, while not as significant as claimed by advocates of the Third Way, were more than cosmetic and cultural.

Neoliberalism reached its peak of political and economic success in the 1990s. Neoliberal globalisation was seen as an unstoppable force, by both enthusiasts (Friedman 1999) and critics (Martin and Schumann 1997).

Social democratic parties were in retreat throughout the world. Financial markets were booming in developed and developing countries alike. The collapse of the Soviet bloc had finally discredited the alternative offered by communism.

The crises of the 21st century

Amid the triumphalism of the 1990s, many predicted that the 21st century would be one of hypercapitalist prosperity. The results have turned out very differently.

The century began with a spectacular crash: the bursting of the US stock market bubble, focussed on 'dotcom' internet stocks, in 2000. The 'dotcom' bubble-and-bust was notable because it occurred at the centre of global capitalism, rather than in peripheral countries where financial capitalism was a recent arrival, as had been the case with the Asian financial crisis of 1997 and earlier emerging market crises.

The expansionary monetary policy allowed a reasonably rapid recovery from the dotcom bust but fuelled a speculative boom, focussed on real estate, that culminated in the GFC of 2008. Far from being the omniscient Masters of the Universe, the financial sector was shown up as corrupt and incompetent. As well as bringing an end to the widely shared prosperity of the 1990s, the stock market collapse undermined the central tenet of neoliberalism, namely, the efficient (financial) markets hypothesis (Quiggin 2011).

The GFC was followed by years of austerity, in which the costs of bailing out the financial sector were borne by the overall population in the form of wage stagnation and reduced public services. Bankers and the financial system were bailed out, while ordinary people were made to pay the price. The situation was worst in the Eurozone, where the design of the ECB made it virtually impossible to adopt any policy except austerity, a counterproductive focus on cutting budget deficits and controlling the non-existent threat of inflation. The result has been a decade of recession in most of the developed world. Even in the USA and the UK, which have, on some measures, recovered, living standards have never returned to the previous growth path, and the inequality of income has been more evident.

Despite its death as a credible theory of economics and politics, however, neoliberalism has stumbled on in zombie form for nearly a decade, maintaining its hold over major political parties and organisations such as the OECD, the IMF and the European Commission. In general, the economics profession has learned almost nothing from the GFC (Quiggin 2013). Ideas like austerity that should have been decently buried long ago continue to wreak havoc throughout the world and, most notably, in Europe (Blyth 2012).

Finally, in 2020, just as the long and grinding recovery from the GFC seemed to be nearing completion, the COVID-19 pandemic smashed the global economy. The management of the pandemic varied from competent to disastrous, but it depended almost entirely on governments. The financial sector played virtually no role on the management of the pandemic but came off unscathed, as usual.

Political implications

Just as the economic ideology of neoliberalism lumbers on in zombie form, so, until recently, has the political system it supported. Insurgents of various kinds have gained support nearly everywhere, but the alternation between different versions of neoliberalism continued for nearly a decade after the crisis, only coming to an end in 2016.

During the decades of neoliberalism that began in the 1970s, the political system, nearly everywhere, was based on electoral competition between the hard and soft versions of neoliberalism, typically represented by (nominally) conservative and social democratic parties, respectively. Within the political class, and among business leaders and policymakers, there was a near-universal consensus in support of neoliberal ideas. To take any position outside the spectrum defined by the soft and hard variants of neoliberalism guaranteed marginalisation and exclusion from serious political debate.

Yet, despite its dominance, neoliberalism hardly ever achieved broad support among the public at large. Rather, the seeming success of neoliberalism concealed the continued strength of currents that remained submerged for decades, becoming politically significant only in occasional eruptions.

The most important of these submerged currents was what may now be called Trumpism, after its most successful exponent (so far). The core of Trumpism is a form of negative or default identity politics best understood using the idea of the 'unmarked category', from linguistics and sociology. Campos (2019) illustrates this:

> An unmarked category is present when the category is considered so normal or ordinary in a particular context that it goes unnoticed. The category is the default setting in regard to social expectations, and it in a sense remains invisible precisely because it is so dominant ... For example, if you had asked a lawyer in 1960 to name three characteristics that every current Supreme Court justice shared, it is very likely the lawyer would not have mentioned either race or gender.

As Campos further observes:

> What 'identity politics', so-called, has done is to slowly and painfully and partially transform being a white man in America into a marked category. And makes a lot of the people who have become white men rather than members of society's invisible default category very uncomfortable.

We may usefully add the unmarked categories 'Christian', where 'Christian' is interpreted in a sense of cultural identification rather than any specific religious belief, and heterosexual, among others.

The most politically potent form of default identity politics, and the relevant one here, is that of a formerly unchallenged dominant group facing the real or perceived prospect of becoming a politically weak and economically declining minority.

Trumpist default identity politics is closely linked to support for 'strongman' rule, exemplified by current practitioners such as Erdogan, Orban, Putin and, of course, Trump himself. This may be because the one universal feature of default identity politics is a worship of masculinity. Theatrical displays of masculinity are a standard feature of Trumpist politics (Trump himself is absurd enough, but Putin's bare-chested horseback rides take these displays to the point of parody and beyond).

During the period of neoliberal dominance, hard neoliberals pandered to Trumpists in rhetorical terms but ignored them wherever their views conflicted with the neoliberal policy agenda, most obviously in relation to trade and migration. Now, the balance has been restored. The Trumpists are in charge but use tax cuts and handouts to favoured cronies to maintain business support.

Opposed to the Trumpists in critical ways, but similar in others, is a disparate group that may be called, for want of a better term 'the left'. As well as a small group who adhere to Marxist or other radical critiques of capitalism, the 'left' in this sense includes environmentalists, feminists, unionists, old-style liberals and social democrats, and a wide variety of groups whose personal or cultural identity is threatened by Trumpism.

Although the left has not been as successful as the Trumpists in political terms, the issues raised by the left, including inequality, racial injustice, gender roles and global heating, have now replaced the concerns of neoliberalism, such as markets and competition, at the centre of the policy agenda for centre-left parties. Rather than advancing a positive agenda of their own, as they did in 1980s and 1990s, the opponents of the left have relied primarily on electoral pragmatism, arguing that a small-target strategy is the best way to election wins.

The way forward

The failure of neoliberalism poses both challenges and opportunities for the left. The greatest challenge is the need to confront Trumpist populism as a powerful political force in itself, rather than as a source of political support for hard neoliberalism. Given the dangers posed by Trumpism, this is an urgent task. One part of this task is that of articulating an explanation of the failure of neoliberalism and explaining why the simplistic policy responses of Trumpist politicians will do nothing to resolve the problems.

The other is to appeal to the positive elements of the appeal of populism, such as solidarity and affection for longstanding institutions, and to counterpose them to the self-seeking individualism central to neoliberalism, particularly in the hard version with which rightwing populism has long been aligned.

The great opportunity is to present a progressive alternative to the accommodations of soft neoliberalism. The core of such an alternative must be a revival of the egalitarian and activist politics of the postwar social democratic moment, updated to take account of the radically different technological and social structures of the 21st century. In technological terms, the most important development is undoubtedly the rise of the internet. Thinking about the relationship between the internet economy and public policy remains embryonic at best. However, the internet, as a massive public good created, in very large measure, by the public sector, ought to present opportunities for a radically remodelled progressive policy agenda.

In political terms, the breakdown of neoliberalism implies the need for a political realignment. This has now taken place on the right, as Trumpists assert their dominance over hard neoliberals. The most promising strategy for the left is to achieve a similar shift in power within the centre-left coalition of leftists and soft neoliberals.

The era of unchallenged neoliberal dominance is clearly over. Hopefully, it will prove to have been a relatively brief interruption in a long-term trend towards a more humane and egalitarian society. Whether that is true depends on the success of the left in putting forward a positive alternative.

Bibliography

Bank for International Settlements (BIS). 2015. 'OTC Derivatives Outstanding'. www.bis.org/publ/otc_hy1605.htm.

Berman, Sheri. 1998. *The Social Democratic Moment: Ideas and Politics in the Making of Interwar Europe*. Cambridge: Harvard University Press.

Blyth, Mark. 2012. *Austerity: The History of a Dangerous Idea*. New York: Oxford University Press.

Boland, Philip J. 1989. 'Majority Systems and the Condorcet jury theorem'. *Journal of the Royal Statistical Society Series D: The* Statistician, 38, no. 3 (September): 181–89. doi.org/10.2307/2348873.

Brenner, Aaron, Robert Brenner, and Cal Winslow, eds. 2010. *Rebel Rank and File: Labor Militancy and the Revolt from Below During the Long 1970s*. New York: Verso Books.

Bump, Philip. 2017. 'Bernie Sanders remains one of America's most popular politicians', *Washington Post*, 15 March 2017. www.washingtonpost.com/news/politics/wp/2017/03/15/bernie-sanders-remains-one-of-americas-most-popular-politicians/?utm_term=.822da5.

Cahill, Damien, and Sharon Beder. 2005. 'Neo-liberal Think Tanks and Neo-liberal Restructuring: Learning the Lessons from Project Victoria and the Privatisation of Victoria's Electricity Industry 2005'. *Social Alternatives* 24, no. 1: 43–48.

Callinicos, Alex. 2001. *Against the Third Way: An Anti-Capitalist Critique.* Cambridge: Polity.

Campos, Paul. 2019. 'Marking the unmarked category', *Lawyers, Guns and Money* (blog). 7 March 2019. www.lawyersgunsmoneyblog.com/2019/03/marking-unmarked-category.

Cavanagh, Matt. 2003. *Against Equality of Opportunity.* Oxford Philosophical Monographs. Oxford: Oxford University Press.

Cockett, Richard. 1995. Thinking the Unthinkable: Think-Tanks and the Economic Counter-Revolution, 1931–1983. London: HarperCollins.

de Condorcet, Nicolas. 1785. *Essay on the Application of Analysis to the Probability of Majority Decisions.* Paris: Imprimerie Royale.

Fama, Eugene. 1970. 'Efficient Capital Markets: A Review of Theory and Empirical Work'. *Journal of Finance* 25 no. 2: 383–417.

Frank, Thomas. 2005. *What's the Matter with Kansas?: How Conservatives Won the Heart of America.* New York: Macmillan.

Friedman, Milton. 1962. *Capitalism and Freedom.* Chicago: University of Chicago Press.

Friedman, Milton. 1968. 'The role of monetary policy'. *The American Economic Review* 58, no. 1 (March): 1–17.

Friedman, Milton, and Rose Friedman. 1980. *Free to Choose: A Personal Statement.* New York: Harcourt Brace Jovanovich.

Friedman, Thomas. 1999. *The Lexus and the Olive Tree: Understanding Globalization.* New York: Farrar, Strauss and Giroux.

Giddens, Anthony. 1998. *The Third Way: The Renewal of Social Democracy.* Cambridge: Polity Press in association with Blackwell.

Giddens, Anthony. 2000. *The Third Way and Its Critics.* Cambridge: Polity Press.

Gordon, Robert J. 2017. *The Rise and Fall of American Growth: The U.S. Standard of Living Since the Civil War.* Princeton: Princeton University Press.

Gruen, Fred and Michelle Grattan. 1993. *Managing Government: Labor's Achievements and Failures.* Melbourne: Longman Cheshire.

Hartwich, Oliver. 2009. 'Neoliberalism: The Genesis of a Political Swearword'. CIS Occasional Paper 114.

Hazledine, Tim and John Quiggin. 2006. 'No More Free Beer Tomorrow? Economic Policy and Outcomes in Australia and New Zealand Since 1984'. *Australian Journal of Political Science* 41, no. 2: 145–59.

Hobsbawm, Eric. 1978. 'The Forward March of Labour Halted?'. *Marxism Today* (September): 279–86.

Humphrys, Elizabeth and Damien Cahill. 2016. 'How Labour Made Neoliberalism'. *Critical Sociology* 43, no. 4–5. doi.org/10.1177/0896920516655859.

Labourcounts. 2023. 'Clause Four Comparisons'. www.labourcounts.com/Clause_four_comparisons.htm.

Marglin, Stephen and Juliet Schor. 1990. *The Golden Age of Capitalism: Reinterpreting the Postwar Experience.* Oxford, New York, Toronto: Clarendon Press.

Martin, Hans-Peter and Harald Schumann. 1997. *The Global Trap: Globalization and the Assault on Prosperity and Democracy.* Translated by Patrick Camiller. London: Zed Books.

Mill, John Stuart. 1848. *Principles of Political Economy.* London: John W. Parker.

Nell, E. 1984. *Free Market Conservatism: A Critique of Theory & Practice.* London: Routledge.

Palley, Thomas. 2013. 'Europe's Crisis Without End: The Consequences of Neoliberalism'. *Contributions to Political Economy* 32 no. 1: 29–50. doi.org/10.1093/cpe/bzt004.

Piketty, Thomas. 2014. *Capital in the Twenty-First Century.* Translated by Arthur Goldhammer. Cambridge: Harvard University Press.

Quiggin, John. 1996. *Great Expectations: Microeconomic Reform and Australia.* St Leonards: Allen & Unwin.

Quiggin, John. 1999. 'The Future of Government: Mixed Economy or Minimal State'. *Australian Journal of Public Administration* 58, no. 4: 39–53. doi.org/10.1111/1467-8500.00126.

Quiggin, John. 2003. 'Word for Wednesday'. *John Quiggin* (blog), 29 January 2003. johnquiggin.com/2003/01/29/word-for-wednesday-2/.

Quiggin, John. 2010. *Zombie Economics: How Dead Ideas Still Walk Among Us.* Paperback Edition. Princeton: Princeton University Press.

Quiggin, John. 2013. 'The State of Economics in 2012: Complacency Amid Crisis'. *Economic Record* 89: 23–30. doi.org/10.1111/1475-4932.12037.

Quiggin, John. 2022. 'The Evolution of Neoliberalism'. In *Sustainability and the New Economics,* edited by Stephen Williams and Rod Taylor. Cham: Springer. doi.org/10.1007/978-3-030-78795-0_6.

Shonfield, Andrew. 1984. *In Defence of the Mixed Economy.* Oxford: Oxford University Press.

Stiglitz, Joseph. 2002. *Globalization and Its Discontents.* New York: W.W. Norton & Company.

Williamson, John. 1990. 'What Washington Means by Policy Reform'. In *Latin American Adjustment: How Much Has Happened?* edited by John Williamson, 7–33. Washington DC: Peterson Institute for International Economics.

Wolfe, Tom. 1987. *The Bonfire of the Vanities.* New York: Farrar, Straus and Giroux.

World Bank. 1993. *The East* Asian *Miracle: Economic Growth and Public Policy.* Oxford: Oxford University Press.

3

Neoliberalism in Australia

Drawn from Quiggin, John. 1996. *Great Expectations: Microeconomic Reform and Australia*. Sydney: Allen & Unwin, Chapter 3.

In many ways, the Australian experience of micro-economic reform parallels the international developments discussed in Chapter 2. An important theme in this chapter is the need to take a sceptical view of arguments suggesting that Australia has had a uniquely poor economic performance and must adopt micro-economic reform policies to catch up with the rest of the world. Nevertheless, it is important to see how the approach taken to micro-economic reform in Australia reflects a response to specifically Australian concerns and to the form of earlier interventionist policies.

The growth of the State in Australia

At least until the Second World War, Australian governments were interventionist by world standards. A number of factors have contributed to this outcome. First, the British colonies in Australia were initially established as combinations of barracks and prisons. It was inevitable that governments should have a dominant role in the development of such societies. Second, the early achievement of an essentially democratic State encouraged the view of government as an instrument for the achievement of shared social goals, rather than as a dangerous power to be hedged around and controlled. Finally, in a huge continent with a small population, only governments had the resources to undertake capital-intensive enterprises such as the construction of railway systems.

As will be argued below, Australia became less distinctive in this respect after the Second World War. In important respects, such as the reliance on tightly targeted flat-rate transfer payment schemes and private superannuation, Australian governments were less inclined to increase outlays than those of other countries in the Organisation for Economic Co-operation and Development (OECD). Thus, by 1994, Australia was, by some measures, the lowest-taxing country in the OECD.[1] The image of an interventionist government in Australia is somewhat out of date.

Nevertheless, a knowledge of the history of government intervention in Australia is important. Although similar reforms have taken place overseas, particularly in other English-speaking countries, the distinctive features of the Australian policy environment have shaped and constrained the course of micro-economic reform. An appreciation of history aids assessment of the debate surrounding micro-economic reform, a central theme of which has been the claim that Australia has been particularly ill-served by its economic institutions and hence is in greater need of radical micro-economic reform than other countries.

The Harvester judgment and the New Protection

With the Federation of Australia in 1901, the role of government was expanded. A vital development was the interaction of the arbitration system governing wages and conditions of employment, and the tariff policy adopted by the federal government. This policy was referred to by its leading advocate, Alfred Deakin, as the New Protection. Under the New Protection policy, tariff protection would be conditional on the payment of adequate wages, with the standard of adequacy being determined on a basis of social need rather than on market criteria. Although attempts to make this conditionality explicit were rejected as unconstitutional, the ideas of the New Protection were effectively implemented in the famous Harvester judgment. In this case, heard in 1907, the Arbitration Court, headed by

---

1   Australia's status as a very low-tax country arises primarily from reliance on private superannuation. The government uses subsidies and the superannuation guarantee levy to ensure widespread participation in the superannuation system, whereas most other OECD countries operate social security systems paying earnings-related retirement benefits. If this difference is discounted, Australia remains a relatively lightly taxed country, but not one of the most lightly taxed.

Justice Henry Higgins, laid down the principle that the basic wage should be sufficient to provide for the needs of a family of five, estimated at 42 shillings a week.

The ideas of the New Protection were given intellectual substance by the report of the Brigden Committee (1929). The committee argued that, while protection yielded a lower per capita income than would free trade, it increased the demand for labour, and, therefore, the size of the population that could be supported at a given real wage, such as that laid down in the Harvester judgment. More generally, this point may be restated as saying that protection of a labour-intensive industry leads to an increase in the equilibrium real wage. This result was formalised as the Stolper–Samuelson theorem (Stolper and Samuelson 1941).

The attempt to secure social equity through the wages system was supported by a series of innovative welfare policies, including age pensions, workers' compensation and the beginnings of a system of unemployment relief. These policies were based on the assumption that families with an employed (male) breadwinner would be adequately protected by the arbitration system and sought to assist those who temporarily or permanently fell outside this group. Thus, it has been described as a 'wage-earners' welfare state' (Castles and Mitchell 1994).

Australian social welfare policies were most distinctive in the period from the Federation to the Great Depression. Hancock's classic study *Australia*, first published in 1930, critically examined features of the political economy of Australia, including tariffs, the arbitration system, public enterprises and the role of the State as a driving force in economic development:

> The Australians have always disliked scientific economics and (still more) scientific economists. They are fond of ideals and impatient of technique. Their sentiments quickly find phrases and their phrases find prompt expression in policies. What the economists call 'law' they call anarchy. The law which they understand is the positive law of the State—the democratic State which seeks social justice by the path of individual rights. The mechanism of international prices, which signals the world's need from one country to another and invites the nations to produce more of this commodity and less of that, belongs to an entirely different order. It knows no rights, but only necessities. The Australians have never felt disposed to submit to these necessities. They have insisted that their governments must struggle to soften them or elude them or master them. (Hancock 1930, 66–67)

It is this set of attitudes that recent advocates of micro-economic reform have set out to overcome. At one level they have been successful. Over the past 20 years, the tariff has been virtually abolished for most industries, the structures of financial regulation have been swept away, public enterprises privatised or prepared for privatisation, and the power of the arbitration system has been greatly reduced. The need to become 'internationally competitive', and the package of policies this implies, is accepted by political leaders of both major parties, by bureaucrats and business leaders, and by the majority of economic commentators.

Yet, on the whole, the Australian public remains unconvinced. The view that governments must struggle to 'soften, … elude … or master' the harsh demands of the marketplace remains part of the Australian ethos.[2] Almost without exception, when the policies of micro-economic reform have been put to the electoral test, they have been rejected.[3] Popular opposition to reform crystallised in the late 1980s around the phrase 'economic rationalism' (Pusey 1991) and does not appear to have abated significantly. In the absence of any clear economic benefits from reform, policies have not been implemented with popular support but have rather been imposed on the basis that 'there is no alternative.'

The clash between public and elite opinion makes the economic assessment of micro-economic reform an issue of more than academic interest. Given the chance, many Australians would willingly turn back the clock of reform. A careful assessment of the gains and losses of micro-economic reform, and of the areas in which reform has succeeded and failed, may help to guide the path of reform and to identify policies that would yield greater benefits to ordinary Australians than the policies adopted in the past.

---

2   The extent to which Australians are unique in this respect may be debated. Henderson (1995) gives an interesting discussion of popular resistance to reform in Australia and abroad.
3   The clearest example is the 1993 federal election, which was a rejection of the Coalition's package of reforms as a whole, including the labour market reform package Jobsback and changes to Medicare. It was not merely a rejection of the proposed goods and services tax (GST). The reforming Greiner government in New South Wales was reduced to a precarious minority status by its first electoral test, and, under the leadership of John Fahey, defeated outright at its second. The defeats of the Field government in Tasmania and the Goss government in Queensland were also due largely to popular hostility to reform. So far, the Kennett government in Victoria is the only reforming state government to have been returned with an outright majority. However, because of the bipartisan commitment to reform, the defeat of one reforming government means nothing more than its replacement by another.

The Australian settlement?

One of the most comprehensive presentations of the case in favour of micro-economic reform is given by Paul Kelly, former editor of *The Australian* newspaper. Kelly (1992) describes what he calls 'the Australian settlement', which he claims dominated Australian society and economic policy from 1901 until the 1980s. Kelly identifies the economic elements of the settlement as consisting of industry protection, arbitration, and State paternalism. He links these economic policies with White Australia and Imperial benevolence, which he initially defines as 'dependence on a great power, (first the UK, then the USA) for its security and finance', but subsequently describes exclusively in terms of attitudes to the UK.[4] Kelly's package represents an extension of the 'Federation trifecta', consisting of protection, arbitration and White Australia, criticised by Henderson (1990).

The link between interventionist economic policies, and the ideas of imperialism and White Australia is misleading. The ideas of White Australia and Imperial benevolence certainly dominated policy up to World War II— the White Australia policy was, in fact, a British Australia policy, and it was regularly claimed that Australia was '98 per cent British' (Hancock 1961, 128). However, the fall of Singapore in 1942 spelled the end of political reliance on the UK, and of Australia's role as a British outpost.

The White Australia policy was undermined by the mass migration programs after World War II, which drew large numbers of southern European migrants, who, before the war, had been regarded as 'a semi-coloured race', to be subject to the most stringent controls (Hancock 1961, 126). Throughout the postwar Keynesian boom, both the White Australia policy and the Imperial connection were steadily eroded. The term 'White Australia' had been officially dropped in 1941, and the end of the policy came in 1966, when both the Liberal–Country Party government and the Labor opposition committed themselves to a non-discriminatory immigration policy.

---

4   If one focusses instead on dependence on the USA, it would be apparent that this aspect of the settlement is alive and well. Indeed, both the blowout in foreign debt and the MX missile crisis, when financial markets fell sharply in response to Australian attempts to assert a limited degree of independence in foreign policy, suggests that financial deregulation reinforced Australia's position as a client state of the USA.

By the early 1970s, when economic interventionism reached its peak, the last vestiges of the White Australia policy were swept away, and the UK, which entered the European Community in 1973, became irrelevant in economic as well as political terms. The link between the White Australia policy, the Imperial connection and interventionist economic policy is long dead. All were widely supported policies of the Federation era, but in the current policy debate, most prominent opponents of micro-economic reform are also opponents of racially discriminatory immigration policies and of a nostalgic emphasis on Britishness. The attempt by advocates of micro-economic reform, such as Kelly and Henderson, to link the policies they oppose with the White Australia policy is a rhetorical device, exploiting the principle of guilt by association.

A more fundamental difficulty with the idea of an Australian settlement put forward by Kelly and Henderson is the failure to take any account of the changes in the political and economic framework brought about by the 30 years of full employment that followed the Second World War (Smyth 1998). No adequate explanation of this exceptional period in our economic history has yet been developed. At the time, however, full employment was seen simply as the result of the adoption of Keynesian macro-economic policies.

The belief that government intervention could guarantee full employment naturally translated into broad confidence in the capacity and responsibility of governments to manage other aspects of the economy. On the other hand, the apparent capacity of fiscal policy to maintain full employment undermined the main rationale for tariff policy as a device for protecting employment. Increasingly, economists came to see tariffs as an indirect and inefficient micro-economic approach to what was properly seen as a macro-economic problem. If anything of value is to be derived from ideas of an Australian settlement, a proper account must be taken of the role of Keynesian full employment policy.

The White Paper and the postwar boom

From World War II onward, Australia's social and economic institutions became more like those of the rest of the developed world. In part, the pressures of the Great Depression forced Australian governments to pay greater attention to the economic logic of the marketplace. Unprofitable state enterprises such as butcher shops and tobacconists were abandoned, and the doctrine that wage rates should be based on an industry's capacity to pay became the central determinant of wage setting. More notably, other countries became more like Australia. Whereas Australia's state-owned railways and public utilities were an exception in the 19th century, by the early postwar period it was the USA's insistence on retaining such enterprises in private ownership that looked exceptional. After World War II, the early Australian experiments with the social welfare system were matched, and on most measures outmatched, by European welfare states.

Nevertheless, the period from 1945 to 1975 was one of steady expansion of the role of government in Australia. The enhanced micro-economic role of government was underwritten by radical changes in macro-economic policy. Australia entered the postwar world with an explicit commitment to the maintenance of full employment, embodied in the 1945 White Paper on Full Employment in Australia. The White Paper was the defining document for economic policy between 1945 and 1975. For the first and possibly the only time, the Australian government accepted an obligation to guarantee full employment and to intervene as necessary to implement that guarantee.

Particularly with respect to trade policy and financial regulation, the perceived demands of macro-economic management overrode any concerns about micro-economic efficiency. A noteworthy example of these priorities was the adoption of quantitative import controls by the Menzies government as a response to balance-of-payments difficulties. At the same time, the apparent success of governments in maintaining stable full employment where markets had failed supported the view that government judgements of social needs were likely to be superior to reliance on market outcomes.

The Liberal–Country Party governments that held office through most of the postwar boom advocated a middle course between the *laissez-faire* doctrines of conservative parties before World War II and the socialist objective proclaimed by the Labor Party. In the intellectual climate of the times, this led to a gradual expansion of the role of government. However, government policy lacked any real coherence or intellectual basis. The advocates of intervention were ill-prepared to meet the critique of their policies advanced by supporters of micro-economic reform from the 1970s onward.

The most notable example was the 'protection all round' policy advocated in particular by the Country Party under Sir John McEwen. In practice, this policy involved assisting the import-competing manufacturing sector and those segments of the rural sector oriented to the domestic market at the expense of the major exporting industries. However, the fact that nearly everyone received some assistance obscured the fundamental point that assistance to one industry is, in effect, a tax on others. It is not surprising that the concept of the 'effective rate of protection' was first developed in Australia. A variety of defences can be advanced for protectionist policies, but 'all round' is difficult, if not impossible, to rationalise.

The Whitlam government

The Whitlam government was elected in 1972 with a program based on a mixture of incompatible elements. On the one hand, at the aggregate level, Whitlam favoured Keynesian macro-economic policies and a substantial expansion of the role of government. On the other hand, the government's stance on tariff policy and, to a lesser extent, with respect to government business enterprises, foreshadowed later developments in micro-economic reform.

Whitlam pursued an essentially free-market industry policy and, indeed, boasted that his was the first genuine free enterprise government in Australian history. The most noteworthy examples of Whitlam's free market approach to industry were the 25 per cent across-the-board tariff cut of July 1973 and the bitterly resented decision to abolish the bounty paid to farmers for purchases of superphosphate. Of more long-term significance was the establishment of the Industries Assistance Commission (later the Industry Commission) in 1973, replacing the old Tariff Board. Since its establishment, the commission has acted as a public advocate of micro-economic reform in every area of the economy.

Another important decision, the significance of which was not recognised at the time, was the abolition of the old Postmaster-General's Department, through which telephone and postal services were supplied, and its replacement by two statutory corporations, Australia Post and Telecom Australia (now Telstra). This decision may be seen in retrospect as the beginning of a process in which large numbers of government services have been first corporatised and ultimately privatised. It should be emphasised, however, that the Whitlam government saw the creation of statutory authorities as a method of increasing the efficiency of public sector provision, and, therefore, of supporting the continued expansion of the public sector.

In other areas of policy, the Whitlam government took a more interventionist stance. It pioneered the imposition of requirements for environmental impact statements. The establishment of the Medibank health insurance system represented a major expansion of direct government involvement in an area where policy had previously been confined to the use of subsidies and tax concessions. Whitlam greatly increased public expenditure and the role of the national government in areas such as education. Most notably, the government's policies with respect to international capital flows were diametrically opposed to its position in favour of free trade in goods. Foreign direct investment was restricted, and devices like the variable deposit requirement were used to control short-term capital flows.

The mixture of interventionist and laissez-faire ideas in the Whitlam program seems intellectually incoherent and has certainly never received an adequate defence. It might be possible to construct such a defence around the idea of a large, but rationally organised, public sector operating in areas characterised by scale economies and externalities, complementing a private sector in which unrestricted competition prevails. But if such an idea is present in Whitlam's defence of his government's record (Whitlam 1985), it is hard to discern.

The retreat of the State since 1975

Despite some important micro-economic reforms, the Whitlam government remained expansionist and interventionist until 1975. In some respects, the Hayden budget of 1975, which embodied a reduction in the budget deficit at a time of high unemployment, may be seen as signalling a retreat from this position. Nevertheless, the era of the retreat of the State began in earnest with the election of the Fraser government.

The Fraser government, 1975–83

The election of the Fraser government in 1975 marked the abandonment of the goal of full employment. Macro-economic policy under Fraser was based on the slogan 'fight inflation first'. Although it was not recognised at the time, the abandonment of the full-employment objective had the effect of undermining government intervention in general, and, hence, of laying the basis for micro-economic reform. More generally, the Fraser government was the first since World War II to translate the traditional Liberal rhetoric of free enterprise into an explicit commitment to cut back the role of government.

Fraser's macro-economic policy focussed primarily on the need to reduce aggregate real-wage levels. This view had some plausibility at the time. Real wages had risen substantially under the Whitlam government. Treasury introduced the concept of the 'real wage overhang', representing the rise in real wages above that which could be justified by productivity growth. Labour market policy under Fraser was dominated by the attempt to drive average real wages down, and, more generally, to weaken the power of the trade unions. The passage of sections 45D and 45E of the *Trade Practices Act 1974*, prohibiting secondary boycotts, certainly had this effect. Although the intention was to restore the authority of the Arbitration Court, sections 45D and 45E have proved useful to employers seeking to bypass arbitration and push through labour market reforms.[5]

Finally, Fraser sought to roll back the growth in government expenditure and taxation that had occurred over the postwar period. Success in this area was limited. Although there was plenty of public support for tax cuts (the 'tax revolt' in the USA dated from this period) and some support for the general idea of reduced government spending, there was little support for specific cuts in expenditure. Moreover, growth in unemployment and in the proportion of the population aged over 65 implied a substantial increase in welfare expenditure without any change in policy.

Although the primary focus of the Fraser government was on retrenchment at the aggregate level, the government undertook several initiatives that may be seen in retrospect as important steps towards micro-economic reform. The most notable was the establishment, in 1979, of the Campbell Committee to inquire into the financial system (the Australian Financial System Inquiry). Progress on implementing the recommendations of the committee, which reported in 1981, was limited by several factors, including the opposition of the Labor Party and the Democrats, who controlled the Senate. Nevertheless, the record of the Fraser government was one of substantial financial deregulation.

---

5   The fact that the push for labour market reform relies heavily on legislation creating new civil and criminal offences, and on the revival of common law offences, underlines the point that the use of the term 'deregulation' is a misnomer.

The Fraser government did not achieve its main objectives. Unemployment fluctuated between 5 and 6 per cent until the 1981–83 recession, when it peaked at above 10 per cent. Although inflation came down from the peaks experienced under the Whitlam government, policies based on control of the money supply failed to deliver a return to the low inflation rates of the 1960s. After some success in cutting back public expenditure as a share of gross domestic product (GDP), the recession of 1981–83 led to a blowout in unemployment benefits and labour market programs.

As a result of this lack of success, and of the government's mixed record on tariff policy, it became fashionable, particularly in Liberal Party circles, to see the Fraser period as a 'missed opportunity' for micro-economic reform. This view, which may be traced back to Henderson (1983), gains some credence from the fact that Fraser himself has emerged as a critic of many aspects of micro-economic reform. Nevertheless, the 'wasted years' view of the Fraser period is essentially anachronistic, since it projects the concerns of a later period back onto the policy debates of the past. At most, this view may be relevant to the government's final term, dominated by the 1981–83 recession. As Kelly (1992, 38) observes:

> It was after 1980 that the radical liberals launched their revolt and the demand grew for free market reforms. It is wrong to attack Fraser for failing to implement these policies in 1976 and 1977 when, frankly, virtually nobody was calling for them.

Even in the period 1980–82, the key disagreements concerned macro-economic policy. Fraser was criticised primarily for resorting to Keynesian expansionary policies in response to the recession that commenced in 1981. Few participants in the policy debate at this time placed much weight on the set of policy issues that were subsequently labelled as micro-economic reform. In subordinating these issues to macro-economic policy concerns, the Fraser government adhered to the economic orthodoxy of the day. As Puplick (private interview 1990, quoted in Kelly 1992, 98) observes: 'A mythology started to be built up by his former close associates about what Fraser had failed to do in office at their urging.'

Most of these points are effectively conceded by Henderson (1994, 256–60).

The myth of 'the wasted years' under Fraser is important, primarily because it gives support to a 'crash through or crash' approach to reform. Any willingness to compromise will, it is argued, open the floodgates to the interest group pressures which were seen as responsible for Fraser's alleged policy weakness. This approach, drawing on public choice theory for additional support, was responsible for the refusal, until it was too late, of former Liberal leader Hewson to compromise on any detail of the *Fightback* program, and therefore ultimately for the Liberals' loss of the 'unlosable' 1993 election.

The Hawke–Keating governments

The election of the Hawke–Keating Labor government in 1983 was a pivotal event in the history of micro-economic reform. During the Fraser government's term of office, the Labor Party had generally opposed reform and advocated a continuation of the policies of the Whitlam era, though with a preference for a slower pace of change and greater attention to economic constraints. The Hawke–Keating government was elected on the basis of a fairly traditional social democratic program, embodied in its 1982 platform. The centrepiece of the platform was the idea of a Prices and Incomes Accord. Although it was subject to flexible interpretation over time, the Accord implied an expansion of the 'social wage' in the form of community services and welfare benefits, and government intervention in the interests of workers, in return for restraint in real and nominal wages.

The first Hawke government took several steps along these lines. However, the leaders of the Labor Party were influenced more and more by the intellectual climate of the time, which strongly favoured micro-economic reform, particularly in the areas of tariff policy and financial deregulation. With the conversion of the leading figures in the government, signalled by the float of the dollar in October 1983, the cause of micro-economic reform had bipartisan support for the first time. Those members of the public opposed to reform, although numerous, had nowhere to go.

The floating of the dollar was a significant step in itself. Acceptance of other micro-economic reforms, and of the general desirability of cutting back the public sector, soon followed. The next important step was made in the Trilogy commitments of 1984. The commitments were:

- Commonwealth tax revenue would not be permitted to grow as a proportion of GDP.
- Commonwealth spending would not grow faster than the economy as a whole.

- The federal deficit would be reduced in money terms in 1985–86 and would not be permitted to grow as a proportion of GDP in the following two years.

From this point on, micro-economic reform proceeded rapidly. The main recommendations of the Campbell Committee were implemented by 1986. By 1988, the government had committed itself to a general reduction in tariffs, and to privatisation of enterprises such as the Commonwealth Bank. In 1990, the two-airlines agreement[6] came to an end, and the basis was laid for competition in telecommunications. During the early 1990s, policies of competitive tendering and contracting out, and private provision of infrastructure, led to a further contraction of the role of government. Most of these policies had bipartisan support and will be continued under the Howard government.

The Hilmer reforms

By 1993, it appeared possible that the movement towards micro-economic reform had lost its momentum. The macro-economic policies that generated the recession had been endorsed by most of the economic commentators and other groups publicly identified with micro-economic reform. The credibility of 'economic rationalism' was gravely reduced as a result. The absence of any substantial payoff from reform in terms of an acceleration in the feasible rate of economic growth was also becoming apparent. The electoral rejection of the *Fightback* package, which embodied a comprehensive program of micro-economic reform, was a reflection of popular hostility to reform. The government, which had reverted to a Keynesian macro-economic stance in the *One Nation* package, was widely suspected of having 'reform fatigue'.

In fact, however, the reform movement quickly regained its strength. The rallying point was the Hilmer Report on competition policy (Hilmer et al. 1993). The report itself was a relatively modest document. It primarily argued that steps should be taken to ensure that government business enterprises do not have unfair advantages in competition with private enterprises. In the policy process arising from the Hilmer Report,

---

6   The two-airlines policy ensured that the two domestic airlines (Ansett, which was privately owned, and TAA, which was publicly owned) offered similar schedules and routes, and prohibited entry by potential competitors.

these principles were extended to their logical conclusions to require a comprehensive program of micro-economic reform, referred to as 'Hilmer and associated reforms'. For example, the principle of fair competition between public and private enterprise was interpreted to require a comprehensive program of competitive tendering and contracting out for publicly provided services.

Implementation of the Hilmer reforms was agreed upon by the state and federal governments meeting as the Council of Australian Governments (COAG) in 1995. The formal results were the passage of the *Commonwealth Competition Policy Reform Act 1995* and the creation of two new bodies: the Australian Competition and Consumer Commission, formed from the amalgamation of the Trade Practices Commission and the Prices Surveillance Authority, and the National Competition Council, a body designed to supervise the progress of federal and state governments towards implementation of competitive reform. More broadly, the COAG process led to a general commitment to apply policies such as competitive tendering and contracting out at all levels of government.

Australia in the OECD context

An important message of this chapter is the need to be wary of particularist accounts in which micro-economic reform is treated primarily as a response to uniquely Australian problems and policy failures. The similarities between Australia and other OECD countries are far more marked than the differences. Like other OECD countries, Australia experienced a long postwar boom, characterised by full employment and expansion of government activity. Again, like other OECD countries, the period since 1975 has been characterised by slow growth, high unemployment and contraction of government activity.

There are, however, important differences between Australia and other countries in the relative emphasis given to different aspects of reform. Micro-economic reform is not a single policy but a vast range of policies affecting different parts of the economy. In any particular case, the Australian experience has differed from that in other countries, and it therefore requires special treatment. However, the general approach adopted here is applicable to other OECD countries, and particularly to the UK and New Zealand, whose policy path has closely resembled the path taken in Australia.

Bibliography

Brigden, JB, DB Copland, EC Dyason, LF Giblin, and CH Wickens. 1929. *The Australian Tariff: An Economic Inquiry*. Melbourne: Melbourne University Press.

Castles, Francis and D Mitchell. 1994. 'An Institutional View of the Australian Welfare State'. *National Strategies Conference* vol. 2, Canberra: Economic Planning Advisory Commission.

Hancock, William K. 1930 [1961]. *Australia*. Brisbane: Jacaranda.

Henderson, D. 1995. 'The Revival of Economic Liberalism: Australia in an International Perspective'. *Australian Economic Review* (1st quarter): 59–85. doi.org/10.1111/j.1467-8462.1995.tb00876.x.

Henderson, G. 1990. *Australian Answers*. Sydney: Random House.

Henderson, G. 1994. *Menzies' Child: The Liberal Party of Australia, 1944–94*. Sydney: Allen & Unwin.

Kelly, P. 1992. *The End of Certainty: The Story of the 1980s*. Sydney: Allen & Unwin.

Pusey, M. 1991. *Economic Rationalism in Canberra: A Nation-building State Changes its Mind*. Cambridge: Cambridge University Press.

Quiggin, John. 1996. *Great Expectations: Microeconomic Reform and Australia*. Sydney: Allen & Unwin, Chapter 3.

Smyth, Paul. 1998. 'Remaking the Australian Way: the Keynesian Compromise'. In *Contesting the Australian Way: States, Markets and Civil Society*, edited by Paul Smyth and Bettina Cass, 81–93. Cambridge: Cambridge University Press.

Stolper, Wolfgang and Paul Samuelson. 1941. 'Protection and Real Wages'. *Review of Economic Studies* 9, no. 1: 58–73. doi.org/10.2307/2967638.

Whitlam, Gough. 1985. *The Whitlam Government, 1972–75*. Melbourne: Penguin.

4

Privatisation and nationalisation in the 21st century

Based on Quiggin, John. 2002. 'Privatisation and Nationalisation in the 21st Century'. *Growth* 50: 66–73.

Introduction

In economic terms, the dominant policy trend of the 20th century was that of nationalisation. In almost all countries and on almost all measures, the range of economic activities undertaken by governments was substantially larger at the end of the 20th century than at the beginning, as was the ratio of public revenue and expenditure to national income.

During the last 20 years of that century, however, there were sustained, and to some extent successful, attempts to roll back the growth of government. Centrally planned economies collapsed and began a transition towards a market-oriented model. In the developed OECD countries, privatisation of publicly owned enterprises took place on a large scale, beginning with the sale by public float of British Telecom, undertaken by the Thatcher government in the UK in 1985.

These developments popularised a triumphalist analysis, in which it was claimed that capitalism had triumphed over socialism, inaugurating the 'end of history' (Fukuyama). This claim was clearly correct if capitalism was understood as the set of economic and political systems prevailing in

OECD countries, ranging from the USA to Norway, and socialism referred to the systems prevailing in the Soviet Union. However, as Fukuyama and subsequent writers such as Friedman (1999) made clear, a much stronger claim was intended. The claim was that history had shown the inevitably of a free-market system similar, in broad terms, to that prevailing in the USA, but with reductions in the role of government along the lines of those proposed in the Republican Party's Contract with America (Gingrich 1994).

Such claims were premature. Although privatisation reduced the role of government in the provision of marketed goods and services, the general government sector (health, education, community services and social welfare) continued to grow in absolute terms and, in many countries, as a proportion of GDP, throughout the 1980s and 1990s. Moreover, by the late 1990s, the pace of privatisation had clearly slowed. For example, in Australia, almost all proposals for privatisation made before 1995 were successful, but in the period after 1995, most were rejected.

In the first years of the 21st century, the rate of privatisation has slowed even further, particularly in Europe and Latin America. More significantly, in the English-speaking countries, a countervailing trend has emerged. For the first time in decades, nationalisation or renationalisation has taken place on a significant scale. Notable examples include the nationalisation of airport security in the USA, the effective renationalisation of the railway system owner Railtrack in the UK and the establishment of a new publicly owned bank in New Zealand.

Transfers

Privatisation and nationalisation frequently involve substantial transfers of wealth. Analysis of these transfers is useful for several purposes. First, it is important to distinguish between transfers of wealth, and efficiency gains or losses, arising from privatisation or nationalisation. Second, analysis of wealth transfers is an important part of any evaluation of welfare effects. Finally, the political economy of privatisation and nationalisation is largely determined by the direction and magnitude of wealth transfers.

Underpricing and buyer overoptimism

The most obvious transfers associated with privatisation by public float, as with private sector initial public offerings (IPOs), arise when the offer price for shares is set at a level below the market value of the shares, as revealed in early trading. In both the private and the public sectors, there are incentives for the organisers of IPOs to set prices below the expected market price, thereby allowing those participating in the float to benefit from first-day 'stag' profits.

First, the negative consequences associated with a 'failed' float (one in which not all shares on offer are taken up) are generally greater than for a float that is oversubscribed. This is particularly true in relation to politically controversial privatisations, where a failure to purchase shares can be represented as a lack of confidence in the government.

Second, the allocation of underpriced shares provides opportunities to give favours to individuals and groups whose goodwill may be valuable in future. Such favours were a prominent and controversial feature of the recent stock-market bubble in the USA. The allocation of discounted shares to employees and others has been a common feature of privatisation in Australia and elsewhere.

Transfers have also arisen in relation to privatisation by trade sale. In many developing and transitional countries, privatisation by trade sale has been the occasion for large-scale expropriation of public wealth. Australian experience has been more favourable, from the viewpoint of the public. Although some assets, such as the New South Wales State Bank, appear to have been sold at unreasonably low prices (Walker and Walker 2000), there have been other instances, such as the sale of Victorian electricity distribution enterprises, where the price paid appeared unreasonably high in the light of the regulatory regime that determined subsequent earnings. In some cases of this kind, such as the privatisation of airports, regulations have been relaxed to allow higher profits, retrospectively validating high sale prices.

Quality of prices and service

The impact of privatisation on prices and service quality has varied, depending particularly on the nature of regulatory changes introduced at the time of privatisation. In general, direct impacts on prices have been small, except where governments have sought to increase the sale price of assets by raising costs to consumers. The most notable recent example was the leasing of Australian airports, which was accompanied by large increases in landing charges (up to 100 per cent) and other charges such as parking fees, and the introduction of a range of new charges, such as taxi levies.

The privatisation of monopolies, when combined with price regulation, has typically led to a reduction in service quality, as monopoly firms seek opportunities to reduce costs and raise profits. Over time, the introduction of steadily more intrusive regulation has reduced both the incentives for lower service quality and the differences in operational efficiency between private and public monopolies.

In some other instances, privatisation has led to the adoption of a more business-like and 'customer-focussed' approach. This has typically been associated with an increase in the quality of service for profitable customers, but also with attempts to discard unprofitable customers and uncompensated community service obligations.

Safety and reliability

Privatisation has generally been accompanied by a decline in the safety and reliability of infrastructure services, particularly when account is taken of exogenous technological trends, which have generally improved the reliability of equipment of all kinds. The cost reductions associated with privatisation and, to a lesser extent, corporatisation, have focussed particularly on reductions in overstaffing in areas such as maintenance, and on the elimination of redundant capital capacity, frequently referred to as 'goldplating'. All things being equal, cost savings achieved in this way must involve some loss of reliability and, in some cases, safety.

The shift from public to private ownership reduces incentives for safety and reliability. The political costs of failures in infrastructure systems can be severe. By contrast, the costs to private infrastructure owners of occasional breakdowns are relatively modest. Hence, if such outcomes are to be avoided, intrusive regulation is likely to be necessary.

Another possible response is the introduction of a legal regime based on the strict liability of infrastructure providers for economic losses associated with system failures. A current class action against Esso in relation to the consequences of the Longford explosion and system failure in Victoria may set a precedent in this respect. Surprisingly, relatively few supporters of the adoption of the US model of private provision of infrastructure services seem to welcome the arrival of a system of regulation in which the threat of litigation plays a central role, as in the USA.

None of the discussion above establishes whether the net impact of reductions in maintenance expenditure is positive or negative. Terms like 'goldplating' and 'redundancy' tend to imply that there is too much reliability, but goldplating makes sense in some contexts (computers) and redundancy in others (aircraft control systems).

Wages, conditions and work intensity

Like other aspects of micro-economic reform, privatisation has imposed costs on workers in the form of increased stress and a faster pace of work. Although anecdotal evidence of increases in work intensity abounds, statistical evidence is limited. The Australian Workplace Industrial Relations Survey undertaken in 1995 found that most employees reported increases in stress, work effort and the pace of work over the previous year, while less than 10 per cent reported reductions in any of these variables (Morehead et al. 1997).

Dawson, McCullough, and Baker (2001, 4) examine the increase in working hours for full-time workers and conclude:

> For many Australian workers, their families and communities, extended working hours have led to increased levels of fatigue and decreasing levels of social support. This in turn has the potential to compromise safety and the long-term health and wellbeing of workers and the organisations that employ them.

Another source of evidence comes from the supply side. The combination of increased work intensity and longer hours of work has rendered full-time employment increasingly unattractive. The full-time participation rate (full-time employment plus those seeking full-time work as a proportion of the population aged between 15 and 64) fell during the 1990s for both males and females. The decline in female participation in the full-time labour force represents the reversal of a long-term trend towards increased participation.

Efficiency gains and losses

Once all transfers to and from workers, consumers and taxpayers have been netted out, the impact of privatisation can be assessed by comparing the value of the enterprise in private ownership, measured by the sale price, with its value in continued public ownership, measured by the present value of the earnings that would have been realised under continued public ownership. The starting point for any such assessment is what may be called the equivalence hypothesis, namely, that in the absence of some specific source of efficiency gains or losses, the value of the asset will be the same in public or private ownership. Hence, in the absence of transfers such as those discussed in the previous section, privatisation will have no effect on the net worth of the public sector (Forsyth 1993).

In this section, a range of possible sources of efficiency gains and losses are considered. Although it is difficult to assess them individually, a market test is provided by a comparison of sale prices with earnings foregone through privatisation.

Operational efficiency

One of the strongest claims for privatisation is that it will increase the operating efficiency, and therefore the profitability, of the enterprises concerned. Empirical studies have yielded mixed results, although the balance of evidence favours the hypothesis that privatisation increases operating efficiency. Borcherding, Pommerehne, and Schneider (1982) surveyed the literature on municipal services and reported that, in most studies, either the private sector was found to be more efficient, or no significant difference was observed. However, in studies of electricity and water services, either the public sector has been found to be more efficient (Pescatrice and Trapani 1980; Bhattacharyya, Parker, and Raffiee 1994), or no significant difference has been discovered (Byrnes, Grosskopf, and Hayes 1986).

Historically, public enterprises have had a wide variety of objectives, and it is reasonable to assume that many of the enterprises in the studies surveyed by Borcherding, Pommerehne, and Schneider (1982) had neither a profit-maximisation objective nor a cost-minimisation objective. One result of this diversity of objectives is the common finding that the variance of performance measures is higher for public than for private firms (Bhattacharyya, Parker, and Raffiee 1994).

A central feature of public sector reform in Australia has been the attempt to replace the diffuse objectives of traditional public enterprises with an objective of profit maximisation subject to the satisfaction of clearly defined community service obligations. This has most commonly been achieved through corporatisation. Corporatised government business enterprises have competed effectively with private firms in many industries, suggesting that any differences in operating efficiency must be modest. It should also be noted that many of the wealth transfers associated with privatisation, such as uncompensated increases in the intensity of work, also arise in corporatised government business enterprises.

Regulatory risk

In some instances, such as cases where governments have owned firms trading in competitive markets, privatisation involves no changes in regulation. However, such cases, typically arising from public rescues of failing firms, have been relatively infrequent. As public ownership expanded during the first 80 years of the 20th century, nationalisation was used primarily as a method of regulating industries that were, or were seen to be, characterised by market failures such as natural monopoly or externality.

In these circumstances, privatisation creates a regulatory risk that does not exist under public ownership. Small differences in the rates of return determined by regulation imply large transfers between consumers and private monopolists. By contrast, under public ownership, this risk is internalised, since, for most regulated infrastructure services, consumers and taxpayers (or, more precisely, residents of the relevant jurisdiction) are the same people.

This analysis directly contradicts a widely held view of public policy in Australia, namely, that there is, in some sense, a conflict of interest in governments both owning and regulating business enterprises. This view lacks any analytical basis. It is analogous to an argument that a conflict arises when a private company contracts with, or directs the actions of, a wholly owned subsidiary.

The costs of regulatory risk are substantial. In Victoria, the failure of private buyers to take regulatory risk into account led to the overoptimistic prices paid for Victorian electricity assets. These purchases have been followed by resales and lower prices, and by vigorous rent-seeking activity aimed at validating the original purchase prices by securing more favourable regulatory treatment.

Cost of capital

The crucial efficiency difference in favour of public ownership arises from differences in the cost of capital. The return demanded by investors in private equity in the average large company includes a risk premium of around six percentage points to compensate for the company's exposure to aggregate economic risk. If the rate of interest on government bonds is 5 per cent, investors in a typical stock will expect a return of around 11 per cent. The equity premium is smaller for companies with stable returns, or for those that are only weakly correlated with the economy as a whole, and larger for those with highly cyclical returns, such as companies involved in construction.

The market's aversion to risk is reflected in the difference between the return demanded by investors in private equity and the rate of return on government bonds or good-quality corporate bonds. This difference is called the equity premium, and its size represents a longstanding puzzle for economists. Most economic models imply that if capital markets spread all relevant risks efficiently and at a low cost, the equity premium should be no more than one percentage point, and probably less. A variety of explanations for the 'equity premium puzzle' have been offered, most of which incorporate the failure of private capital markets to spread risk as well as is assumed in neoclassical models of the financial sector.

As Grant and Quiggin (2003) observe, if the demand for a high rate of return on equity arises from failures in private capital markets, there is no reason to apply this rate of return in evaluating public investments or determining the present value of income streams flowing from government business enterprises.

An assessment of Australian privatisations

As has been argued in this paper, the effects of privatisation can be assessed by examining the difference between the sale price realised for an asset and the present value of earnings foregone under public ownership, after netting out transfers to and from workers, consumers and buyers of assets. Such analyses of actual and prospective privatisations have been performed for the Commonwealth Bank (Quiggin 1995), Commonwealth Serum Laboratories (Hamilton and Quiggin 1995), Telstra (Quiggin 1996a), the New South Wales State Bank (Walker and Walker 2000) and the Victorian electricity industry (Quiggin 2002a), among others.

In all cases, the analysis indicated a net welfare loss from privatisation. In the case of Victorian electricity, however, the loss was borne by the buyers (mainly US electricity companies) who paid prices that were, at least in retrospect, excessive. Hence, the net impact on Victorian residents was roughly neutral, with gains to taxpayers being offset by losses to workers and consumers.

Based on this evidence, it seems unlikely that the privatisation of efficiently run government business enterprises in core areas of government activity such as infrastructure is ever likely to be beneficial, except during market bubbles, when buyers may be willing to pay prices that exceed the long-run private market value of assets.

The case for renationalisation

Thinking the unthinkable

Until about 1980, the idea of a substantial reduction in the scale and scope of public sector economic activity lay outside the realm of acceptable public debate. Cockett's (1995) classic study of the British think tanks that first advocated privatisation, such as the Institute for Economic Affairs, was aptly titled *Thinking the Unthinkable*. Such is the power of conformism in human affairs that within a decade of its entry into the public debate, the insurgent idea of privatisation had become an orthodox dogma, and the concept of nationalisation was, literally, unthinkable for many.

This point may be illustrated with reference to the Australian debate. Criticisms of privatisation, such as those of Quiggin (1995) and Walker (1994), have been the subject of vigorous debate (Hathaway 1997; Officer 1999). However, until recently, arguments that the appropriate response to the failures of privatisation is a return to public ownership (Quiggin 2000) have simply been ignored.

This position is slowly changing, although the public debate is lagging behind events in the real world. Renationalisation in various forms has taken place in numerous countries, sometimes as a deliberate attempt to offset excessive privatisation, but more frequently in response to the failures of privatised firms and the associated regulatory structure.

71

In Australia, Minister for Small Business Joe Hockey recently suggested that it might be necessary for state governments to re-enter the insurance business following the collapse of HIH Insurance and United Medical Protection. The unthinkable is becoming thinkable once again.

The mixed economy

In most OECD countries, governments, and government business enterprises, produce around 30 per cent of total output. This proportion has tended to grow over time, reflecting the increasing economic importance of the sectors in which government activity is concentrated, such as health and education. Large-scale privatisation has offset or reversed the trend towards a larger government sector in several countries, including the UK. Nevertheless, it seems clear that, for the foreseeable future, OECD countries will have mixed rather than free-market economies.

In a mixed economy, even supporters of further privatisation should welcome the availability of nationalisation as a policy option. If privatisation is, as is sometimes supposed, irreversible, it should be undertaken with great caution. By contrast, if both privatisation and nationalisation are feasible, it is possible to adjust the boundary between the private and public sectors optimally in response to new information and changed circumstances.

Nevertheless, the policy relevance of nationalisation is greatest in cases in which privatisation has already gone too far. The evidence cited in this paper suggests that this is the case in Australia, and that a number of privatisations already undertaken have reduced both public sector net worth and the welfare of the community as a whole. It follows that, in the absence of transactions costs, renationalisation would improve welfare.

Targets for renationalisation

The strongest candidate for renationalisation in Australia at present is Telstra. Even supporters of privatisation, such as Treasurer Peter Costello, agree that the current state of partial privatisation is highly unsatisfactory. When the current government's proposal for partial privatisation was under consideration, the same view was expressed in Quiggin (1996b) and derided by members of the government. On the other hand, given Telstra's monopoly power, full privatisation would be acceptable to other market participants only if it was accompanied by more stringent regulation. The implied regulatory risk reduces the market value of Telstra, which is well below any reasonable estimate of the value of future real earnings, discounted at the real bond rate.

The privatisation of Telstra could be financed in part by the sale of peripheral assets, such as Telstra's pay-TV interests and joint ventures in Hong Kong. This idea, along with proposals for more extensive structural separation, has been discussed by Quiggin (2002b) and Tanner (2002), and criticised by Eason (2002).

Renationalisation of infrastructure assets that have been fully privatised is further off, except in cases such as that of Railtrack, in which the private operator fails completely. Nevertheless, it would be highly desirable to restore full public ownership of the road system and to replace the present arbitrary patchwork of tolls with a rational system of road-user charging. Less urgent, but still highly desirable, is the renationalisation of natural monopoly infrastructure such as water supply in South Australia, and electricity distribution in South Australia and Victoria.

Concluding comments

The limitations and failures of privatisation are widely recognised, but the obvious implication—namely, that at least some privatised enterprises should be renationalised—remains unthinkable for many. Thus far, renationalisation has occurred primarily as an emergency response to the failure of private firms providing essential services. As instances of this kind break down the notion that privatisation is irreversible, it may be possible to undertake a more systematic and rational reconsideration of the appropriate roles of the public and private sectors.

Bibliography

Bhattacharyya, Arunava, Elliott Parker, and Kambiz Raffiee. 1994. 'An Examination of the Effect of Ownership on the Relative Efficiency of Public and Private Water Utilities'. *Land Economics* 70, no. 2: 197–209. doi.org/10.2307/3146322.

Borcherding, Thomas, Werner Pommerehne, and Friedrich Schneider. 1982. 'Comparing the Efficiency of Private and Public Production: The Evidence from Five Countries'. Supplement 2, *Zeitschrift für Nationalökonomie / Journal of Economics*: 127–56.

Byrnes, Patricia, Shawna Grosskopf, and Kathy Hayes. 1986. 'Efficiency and Ownership: Further Evidence'. Review of *Economics and Statistics* 68 (May): 337–41. doi.org/10.2307/1925517.

Cockett, Richard. 1995. Thinking the Unthinkable: Think-Tanks and the Economic Counter-Revolution 1931–1983. London: HarperCollins.

Dawson, Drew, Kirsty McCulloch, and Angela Baker. 2001. *Extended Working Hours in Australia: Counting the Costs*. Woodville: Centre for Sleep Research, University of South Australia.

Eason, Ros. 2002. 'What Role for Telstra?'. Evatt Papers 41, Evatt Foundation.

Forsyth, Peter. 1993. 'Privatisation: Private Finances and ublic Policy'. In *Privatisation: The Financial Implications,* edited by Kevin Davis and Ian Harper, 8–22. St Leonards: Allen and Unwin.

Friedman, Thomas. 1999. *The Lexus and the Olive Tree: Understanding Globalization*. New York: Farrar Strauss and Giroux.

Fukuyama, Francis. 1992. *The End of History and the Last Man*. New York: The Free Press.

Gingrich, Newt. 1994. *Contract with America*. New York: Republican National Committee.

Grant, Simon and John Quiggin 2003. 'Public Investment and the Risk Premium for Equity'. *Economica* 70, 1–18. www.jstor.org/stable/3548814.

Hamilton, Clive, and John Quiggin. (1995). 'The Privatisation of CSL'. Discussion paper no. 4, The Australia Institute, Canberra, June 1995.

Hathaway, Neville. 1997. 'Privatisation and the Government Cost of Capital'. *Agenda* 4, no. 1: 1–10. doi.org/10.22459/ag.04.02.1997.03.

Morehead, Alison, Mairi Steele, Michael Alexander, Kerry Stephen, and Linton Duffin. 1997. *Changes at Work: The 1995 Australian Workplace Industrial Relations Survey*. Melbourne: Addison Wesley Longman Australia.

Officer, Robert. 1999. 'Privatisation of public assets'. In *Privatisation: Efficiency of Fallacy? Two Perspectives*, edited by CEDA (Committee for Economic Development of Australia): 1–22.

Pescatrice, Donn and John Trapani III. 1980. 'The Performance and Objectives of Public and Private Utilities Operating in the United States'. *Journal of Public Economics* 13: 259–76. doi.org/10.1016/0047-2727(80)90016-x.

Quiggin, John. 1995. 'Does Privatisation Pay?'. *Australian Economic Review* 28 no. 2: 23–42. doi.org/10.1111/j.1467-8462.1995.tb00886.x.

Quiggin, John. 1996a. *The Partial Privatisation of Telstra: An Assessment*. Submission to Senate Environment, Recreation, Communications and the Arts Reference Committee Inquiry into the Telstra (Dilution of Public Ownership) Bill 1996.

Quiggin, John. 1996b. 'Partial Sale: "Worst of All Options"', *Communications Update* 119: 4–5.

Quiggin, John. 2000. 'Why Nationalise?'. Paper presented to The Economic Society of Australia Conference, Adelaide.

Quiggin, John. 2002a. 'The Fiscal Impact of the Privatisation of the Victorian Electricity Industry'. *The Economic and Labour Relations Review* 13, no. 2: 326–39. doi.org/10.1177/103530460201300209.

Quiggin, John. 2002b. 'Telstra: the case for renationalisation and divestiture'. *Evatt News* 75. Evatt Foundation.

Quiggin, John. 2002c. 'Privatisation and Nationalisation in the 21st Century'. *Growth* 50: 66–73.

Tanner, Lindsay. 2002. 'Reforming Telstra'. *ALP Telstra Discussion Paper* (23 May 2022). library.fes.de/aussies/2002/0502/20001060.html.

Walker, Robert. 1994. 'Privatisation: A Re-assessment'. *Journal of Australian Political Economy* 34: 27–52.

Walker, Robert and Betty Walker. 2000. *Privatisation: Sell Off or Sell Out?: The Australian Experience*. Sydney: ABC Books.

5

Looking back on micro-economic reform: a sceptical viewpoint

First published in 2004 as Quiggin, John. 'Looking Back on Microeconomic Reform: A Sceptical Viewpoint'. *Economic and Labour Relations Review* 15: 1–25. doi.org/10.1177/103530460401500101.

The era of micro-economic reform in Australia began with a big bang—the floating of the dollar in 1983. It ended with another big bang—the package of tax reforms centred on the goods and services tax (GST), which came into force in July 2000. The period between 1983 and 2000, roughly corresponding to the 1980s and 1990s, was one of systematic, though gradual, micro-economic reform affecting nearly all sectors of the economy.

There were isolated instances of micro-economic reform before the 1980s, notably including the Whitlam government's 25 per cent tariff cut (the primary motive here was macro-economic, but the choice of instrument reflected micro-economic concerns). Similarly, the consequences of some micro-economic reforms initiated in the 1990s, such as the National Competition Policy, are still being worked through, and a few items on the micro-economic reform agenda, such as the full privatisation of Telstra, are still being debated. Moreover, movement in the direction of micro-economic reform was never uniform. The Prices and Incomes Accord constituted a major change in the way Australian labour markets operated but was not generally considered as an instance of micro-economic reform.

Despite these qualifications, the 1980s and 1990s can reasonably be characterised as the era of micro-economic reform in Australia. Throughout this period, there was a steady movement in the direction of micro-economic reform, backed by a bipartisan, and almost monolithic, intellectual consensus, at least among policy elites. No such consensus existed before the 1980s.

Most economic evaluations of micro-economic reform in Australia and elsewhere, particularly those from official sources, have been favourable. Parham (2002b) is a good recent example. In light of this favourable evaluation, there have been calls for a renewed commitment to micro-economic reform (Dawkins and Kelly 2003). On the other hand, it is widely recognised that the Australian public is suffering from reform fatigue and evinces little support for further micro-economic reform. Given that the public has had two decades to evaluate the effects of micro-economic reform, these observations pose a problem. Either the official estimates of the benefits of micro-economic reform are overoptimistic, or members of the public have consistently misperceived the effects of reform on their welfare.

The object of this paper is to present a sceptical evaluation of micro-economic reform in Australia, without an initial presumption that reform is either beneficial or harmful. The paper is organised as follows. Definitions of the concept of 'micro-economic reform' are discussed, and the policy agenda associated with this term is described. I distinguish several phases of micro-economic reform, then evaluate the program of micro-economic reform according to several criteria, including impacts on macro-economic performance, allocative efficiency, productivity, work intensity and consumer choice. Finally, I offer some concluding comments.

Defining micro-economic reform

Although micro-economic reform is notoriously difficult to define, the central idea is that policy should be directed to achieving improvements in economic efficiency, either by removing distortions in individual sectors of the economy or by reforming economy-wide policies, such as tax policy and competition policy, with an emphasis on economic efficiency (rather than other goals such as equity or employment growth).

Considering the term 'micro-economic reform' in more detail, the 'micro-economic' element is significant in two ways. First, the shift to a focus on micro-economic reform represented an acknowledgement that macro-economic policies, and particularly Keynesian demand management, were no longer as effective as they had appeared to be during the long postwar boom. Micro-economic reform was seen by some of its advocates as a way of removing structural barriers to the effectiveness of macro-economic policy. Other advocates of micro-economic reform, influenced by new classical models, saw little role for macro-economic policy and argued that the main task of economic reform was to remove the distortions created by previous interventionist policies.

The term 'reform' literally means 'change of form'. However, in its positive uses, it embodies two additional connotations. The first is 'change for the better'. The second is the idea of change that is, in some sense, historically inevitable. Both of these elements were present in discussions of micro-economic reform, particularly in the wake of the collapse of communism, and were embodied in the slogan attributed (perhaps apocryphally) to Margaret Thatcher: 'There is No Alternative'. A more sophisticated version of the same claim was made by Fukuyama (1992). Critics of micro-economic reform, who had often been supporters of interventionist economic policies that were also described as reforms at the time they were implemented, initially resisted the use of the term 'reform' to describe policies they regarded as producing changes for the worse. However, the term 'micro-economic reform' is now used in much the same way by supporters, opponents and sceptics alike.

Micro-economic reform may be defined as a systematic program of reform along market-oriented lines and focussing on micro-economic issues rather than macro-economic policy.

In light of this discussion, the statement made above that 'the Prices and Incomes Accord … is not typically considered as an instance of micro-economic reform' can be clarified. The Accord does not meet the definition of micro-economic reform, partly because it was motivated by macro-economic concerns, and partly because it sought to produce outcomes different from those that would be generated by market forces.

More generally, according to this definition, there was no systematic commitment to micro-economic reform before 1983, despite some policy initiatives consistent with the ideas underlying such reform. Similarly, Australian state and national governments are no longer pursuing systematic programs of micro-economic reform.

International experience

Although the specific term 'micro-economic reform' is most popular in Australia, closely related policies were pursued throughout much of the world in the 1980s and 1990s, commonly described in such terms as 'structural reform'. The policies adopted in Australia were largely modelled on those of the Thatcher government in the UK, which were also emulated in New Zealand and Canada. Radical market-oriented reforms were adopted in eastern Europe and Russia after the collapse of communism, accelerating an earlier, more gradual trend towards a larger role for the market. Under pressure from agencies such as the World Bank and the IMF, many less developed countries also abandoned interventionist policies, such as import replacement and public ownership, and embraced policies of liberalisation and privatisation.

The debate over whether the effects of reform have been beneficial or harmful on balance has yielded little in the way of firm conclusions. This is unsurprising given the potential for disagreement over criteria, counterfactuals and measurement criteria, which will be discussed in more detail with respect to Australia.

Nevertheless, some countries have clearly performed better than others. For example, Australia has outperformed New Zealand. This fact has given rise to a debate over reform strategies, which has focussed on two main issues. The first is the choice between radical restructuring (sometimes referred to as shock therapy) and gradual reform. Among advocates of gradual reform, there is a further debate about sequencing. The issue is whether it is preferable to delay some reforms to a later stage of the reform process and, if so, which (Bollard and Buckle 1987).

The micro-economic reform agenda

The term 'micro-economic reform' encompasses a wide range of policies, and the content of the micro-economic reform agenda has changed over time. Nevertheless, in most periods, one or two central themes have dominated the policy agenda.

Getting prices right

In the early phases of micro-economic reform, much attention was focussed on 'getting prices right' and, in particular, on eliminating policies that unnecessarily 'distorted' the production and consumption decisions of private firms and households. The paradigmatic example of a 'distorting' policy was tariff protection. The case for tariff reform was bolstered by the argument that, if a government wished to assist particular industries, it should do so through subsidies, which did not distort the prices faced by consumers.

Under the policy of 'protection all round', the impact of tariffs on agricultural producers had been partially offset by a range of price stabilisation and support policies. The gradual removal of these policies began with the Whitlam government's controversial abolition of a bounty on purchases of superphosphate and the 25 per cent cut in tariffs, introduced in July 1973.

The consensus in favour of 'protection all round' had marginalised both advocates of the traditional free-trade alternative to protection, and supporters of strategic industry policies and micro-economic planning. As a result, advocates of more comprehensive and systematic government intervention, such as Whitlam, initially made common cause with those who favoured extensive free-market reform. Both groups were classed as 'economic rationalists'[1], that is, advocates of rationally designed policy, as opposed to the advocates of the status quo, in which policy was driven by a mixture of historical precedent, lobbying, and ad hoc responses to crises. Under the Fraser government, the free-market element of economic rationalism became dominant, and the term came to imply a desire to reduce the role of government, rather than, as under Whitlam, to apply the power of government more rationally and systematically. Much later, following the popular critique of Pusey (1991), 'economic rationalist' acquired a primarily pejorative connotation.

Under the case-by-case approach pursued during the 1970s, proposals for tariff reform were initially most successful in industries with relatively low protection. In the highly protected industries most threatened by import competition, such as motor vehicles and textiles, clothing and footwear, tariffs were supplemented by quotas. As a result, the variance of effective

---

1   For further discussion of the genesis of the term 'economic rationalism', see Quiggin (1997a). and Schneider (1998).

rates of protection increased substantially during the 1970s, as shown in Table 5.1. The first two rows of data show the mean and variance of tariff rates from 1971 to 1991.

Table 5.1 Effective rates of protection (%) 1971–91

	1971	1973	1983	1988	1991
Mean effective protection rate	36	27	25	19	15
Standard deviation of effective protection rates	25	20	43	36	29

Source: Industry Commission

It was not until 1988 that the case-by-case approach was replaced by a general program of reducing tariff rates across the board, a process that is still incomplete.

Corporatisation and privatisation

A second strand of micro-economic reform focussed on improving the efficiency of government business enterprises. One of the first, and most successful, instances was the creation of the statutory authorities Australia Post and Telecom Australia from the former Postmaster-General's Department, a public service department under direct ministerial control. More generally, the reform of government provision of marketed services may be seen in terms of a spectrum. At one end is the traditional departmental structure of national, state and local governments. At the other end is a privatised firm, subject only to normal commercial regulation. The points on the spectrum include:

1. full cost pricing
2. competitive tendering
3. commercialisation
4. corporatisation
5. privatisation.

Each step along the reform spectrum involves an increase in reliance on profit as the primary guide to management decisions, and a reduction in direct public accountability. These two changes are directly linked: increases in profitability arise precisely because managers are not subject to constraints imposed through public accountability and are therefore free to manage enterprises so as to increase revenues and reduce costs.

From the perspective of advocates of micro-economic reform, the object of reform has been to move as far towards privatisation as possible, subject to constraints arising from potential market failures or political restrictions. Under the National Competition Policy (NCP), traditional arrangements are considered, prima facie, to be anti-competitive, and governments are required to consider options such as commercialisation and corporatisation.

For much of the 1980s and 1990s, it seemed that movement along the reform spectrum led inexorably to full privatisation. By the late 1990s, however, political resistance to privatisation had hardened. A central element in the decline of support for privatisation was the realisation that the budgetary arguments that had been used to justify early privatisations in Australia and the UK were spurious. The budgetary conventions prevailing until the mid-1990s allowed the proceeds of asset sales to be treated as current revenue or, in some cases, negative expenditure.

In assessing the fiscal impacts of privatisation, the appropriate comparison is between the sale price and the present value of income foregone as a result of privatisation. In most cases, if this comparison is undertaken using the real bond rate as a discount rate, sale proceeds are less than the present value of earnings foregone on any reasonable estimate (Quiggin 1995; Walker and Walker 2000). The divergence is primarily due to the 'equity premium', that is, the difference between the real rate of interest on bonds and the rate of return demanded by investors in private equity. This difference, about six percentage points on most estimates, is too large to be consistent with the standard consumption-based capital asset-pricing model, under which asset prices are determined by consumers rationally optimising the expected utility of lifetime consumption in efficient asset markets (Mehra and Prescott 1985; Kocherlakota 1996).

Moreover, the equity premium is independent of any divergences in public and private discount rates arising from differential taxation treatment and from transfers that may be associated with underpricing in cases of privatisation by public float. Differences arising from the latter sources should be netted out in the evaluation of privatisation.

There are strong grounds for supposing that observed market imperfections, such as transaction costs in household borrowing and lending (Constantinides, Donaldson, and Mehra 1998), and the absence of insurance markets for systematic risks such as unemployment and business failure (Mankiw 1986; Weil 1989; Grant and Quiggin 2002), play an important role in explaining the anomalously large equity premium. If so, as Grant and Quiggin (2003) observe, the appropriate discount rate for evaluating privatisation is likely to be close to the real bond rate, implying that most Australian privatisations have reduced welfare.

Supporters of privatisation have argued for a presumption in favour of the market rate (Hathaway 1997) or have sought to change the focus of the argument away from fiscal impacts to broader efficiency effects (Officer 1999). In the absence of evidence supporting the use of the market rate, the first position is purely ideological. As regards the second, it is important to take account of impacts on consumers, employees and others. However, assuming the sale price is equal to the private market value of earnings under privatisation, a comparison of this sale price with the present value of expected earnings under continued public ownership captures the main efficiency effects of privatisation.

Deregulation and reregulation

The first big instance of deregulation in Australia was the deregulation of financial markets in the 1980s, following the recommendations of the Campbell and Martin Committees of Inquiry and the decision to float the Australian dollar in 1983. Deregulation of the airline industry, and the abandonment of the long-standing two-airlines policy, followed in 1990.

Reforms to telecommunications and energy markets in the 1990s are also commonly referred to as deregulation. In these cases, in which a relatively simple, although highly restrictive, regulatory regime, based on publicly owned statutory monopolies, has been replaced by a complex set of regulations designed to facilitate competition, 'reregulation' might be a more appropriate term. Continued use of the term 'deregulation' reflects, in part, the idea that the new regulatory structures are interim measures, paving the way for the emergence of a fully competitive market.

Measured against the, admittedly ambitious, objective of a competitive outcome requiring only the basic regulatory functions of standard company law, deregulation in Australia has been almost uniformly unsuccessful. In banking, the position of incumbent firms has been strengthened, most notably by mergers allowed in anticipation of deregulation. Entry by foreign banks, regarded *ex ante* as the main source of competition, has been limited and transient. Competition has been further reduced by the virtual disappearance of the building society sector when the regulatory costs of a banking licence were removed, while the implicit Commonwealth government guarantee, arising from the Reserve Bank's role as lender of last resort, remained in place. This trend has been partially offset by the emergence of non-bank mortgage originators in the 1990s.

The abolition of the two-airlines policy induced a number of competitors to enter the market from 1990 onwards. The first two entries, both using the name Compass, were costly failures. Although external factors such as the first Gulf War played a role, the entrants were poorly capitalised, and there were extensive barriers to entry, notably including the incumbents' control of terminals. Pressure to liberalise access to terminals developed in the wake of the Compass failures, but the incumbents built up alternative barriers to entry such as frequent flyer schemes. Several other enterprises announced plans to enter the market during the 1990s but failed to secure the necessary finance. A third failure was the attempt by regional airline Impulse to enter the capital city market, beginning in 2000. Shortly after Impulse commenced service, the fourth (and so far the only successful) entrant, Virgin Blue, also entered the market. Unlike previous entrants, Virgin Blue had the backing of an international carrier.

The success of Virgin's entry depended on a series of adverse events that had fatally weakened one of the incumbent airlines, Ansett. The last of these was the terrorist attack of September 11, 2001, which occurred immediately after Ansett's declaration of bankruptcy and ensured that attempts to refloat the airline would not succeed. Thus, the competitive entry of Virgin has resulted in the replacement of the symmetrical duopoly imposed under the two-airline policy with a Stackelberg leader–follower model, in which the dominant firm (the leader) sets the conditions under which its rival (the follower) competes.

The outcome in the telecommunications sector has been similar, with Telstra acting as a Stackelberg leader. Of course, this outcome represents an increase in competition relative to the starting point of statutory monopoly. Similarly, in the electricity sector, although there are more firms than before, most retail consumers are effectively dealing with monopolists.

Even under the more limited criterion of reductions in prices, success has been limited. The interest rate margins charged by banks to household customers rose in the aftermath of the speculative boom and bust of the 1980s. Although margins have subsequently fallen, this has been offset by a steady increase in fees and charges.

Business class and standard economy airfares have generally risen, but the proportion of discount fares and the size of discounts have increased. Using an index number approach, Quiggin (1997b) concluded that there had been no significant change in the cost of a standard basket of airfares, consisting of a mixture of business-class, full economy and discount fares. Forsyth (1998) criticised the claim that discount fares should be treated as a separate commodity and concluded that average fares had fallen as a result of deregulation. Bailey (2003) finds little change in prices between 1992 and 2003.[2]

Prices of telecommunications services have fallen in real terms, but this reduction has merely continued a trend that prevailed throughout the 20th century. More precisely, the regulatory constraints on Telstra's prices embody a requirement to continue the rate of price reductions observed before the advent of competition. In most years, this constraint has been binding, implying that the aggregate impact of reregulation on prices has been zero. As with airlines, there has been a redistributive effect. Consumers with more elastic demand and lower marginal costs of service have benefited at the expense of those with less elastic demand and higher marginal costs. In this case, unlike that of airlines, the redistribution has generally favoured business at the expense of households. (In both cases, it must be assumed that reductions in business costs ultimately flow through to households.)

The most striking single outcome of deregulation was the speculative boom and bust in equity markets in the 1980s, the magnitude of which was largely attributable to financial deregulation. The rise of 'entrepreneurs' engaged in speculative takeovers was widely seen as a positive outcome of financial deregulation, imposing market discipline on lazy incumbent managers (Bishop, Dodd, and Officer 1987). In retrospect, however, it is apparent that the entrepreneurs had little capacity to improve the value of the enterprises they controlled and primarily illustrated the maxim, attributed to JK Galbraith, that 'genius is a rising market'. When equity prices declined after 1987, the corporate structures built up by the entrepreneurs collapsed with heavy losses.

---

2   A more relevant comparison would be the change in airfares compared to that which would have taken place under continued regulation. Presumably, this would have been relatively modest over the short period assessed by Quiggin and Forsyth, but it might have been significant over the 1990s as a while.

No accurate estimate of the welfare loss associated with this episode has been made. However, Sykes (1994) estimates the volume of losses incurred by creditors and bondholders at A$20 billion or around 5 per cent of annual GDP in the 1980s.[3] As was noted by Milbourne and Cumberworth (1991), much of this loss was transferred to retail customers of the banks in the form of increased margins between borrowing and lending rates.

Another substantial welfare loss arose from the parallel rollouts of hybrid fibre optic cable undertaken by Telstra and Optus in the mid-1990s. At a cost greater than would have been incurred in an orderly rollout of cable for all metropolitan areas, Telstra and Optus produced two sets of cables, each covering about half the population, with an overlap estimated at 90 per cent. The total welfare loss was at least A$4 billion and possibly as much as A$8 billion (1 to 2 per cent of GDP).

Against these losses must be set improvements in operating efficiency, associated with reductions in overstaffing and the elimination of restrictive work practices. Based on observed changes in prices, the net impact appears to be about neutral in the case of telecommunications and airlines. On the other hand, as noted above, financial deregulation produced a substantial welfare loss in its first decade from 1983 to 1993. Outcomes since 1993 appear more favourable, but a final evaluation must await the end of the current economic cycle.

Competition and competition policy

During the 1990s, the process of micro-economic reform changed radically, as did its content. Increasing public resistance to policies such as privatisation, combined with an upsurge of hostility to 'economic rationalism' in general, made it difficult to implement reform through political processes, except in a crisis atmosphere such as that following the collapse of state banks in Victoria and South Australia.

As a result, reform in the 1990s was often implemented without open political debate. The most notable example was the NCP, which grew out of the report of the Hilmer Committee (Hilmer, Rayner and Taperell

---

3   Since other losses were incurred by employees, customers and others, this is likely to be a lower-bound estimate of welfare costs. On the other hand, in a complete analysis it would be necessary to take account of gains to entrepreneurs. Despite most of the leading entrepreneurs having incurred personal as well as corporate bankruptcy, it appears that a number of them managed to retain significant personal wealth after the crash, in addition to consumption expenditure during the boom in housing prices.

1993), appointed in 1992 to inquire into, and advise on, appropriate changes to legislation and other measures in relation to the scope of the *Trade Practices Act 1974* and the application of the principles of competition policy. Advocates of reform within federal government policy circles used the Hilmer Report as the basis for a renewed push for public sector reform, centred around the Council of Australian Governments (COAG).

By virtue of its reliance on intergovernmental negotiations and remoteness from open political debate, the COAG process permitted further extensions of reform to be presented as a fait accompli, embodied in the *Commonwealth Competition Policy Reform Act 1995* and the associated Competition Principles Agreement. By the time its implications were realised, the NCP was both Commonwealth and state law, backed up by the power of the National Competition Council (NCC) to penalise recalcitrant or tardy states.

This process in turn produced a counter-reaction, in which NCP became a scapegoat for all the adverse consequences of micro-economic reform and for many trends independent of that reform. A typical example was the closure of banks in country towns, which was due in part to financial deregulation and in part to long-standing demographic trends but had nothing to do with NCP.

The NCP program had three main components. The first was a once-off review of all state and federal legislation, requiring that any legislation with anti-competitive effects should be justified on the grounds of public benefit. A notable outcome was the deregulation of the dairy industry, discussed by Edwards (2003). The second was a requirement for government business enterprises to adopt prices based on the principle of 'competitive neutrality'. The third, and in the end the most significant, was the creation of a new system of regulatory oversight for public and private enterprises declared as monopolies.

At least at first sight, it may appear paradoxical that the ultimate outcome of NCP was a substantial expansion of regulation. The implementation of NCP required the establishment of the NCC and the formation of a more powerful Australian Competition and Consumer Commission (ACCC) from the former Trade Practices Commission and Prices Surveillance Authority. In addition, each of the states established regulatory bodies. In one sense, this expansion of regulation represents a retreat from the original aspirations of advocates of micro-economic reform, who hoped to replace government monopolies with competitive markets. In most cases, it has now been recognised that the core functions historically performed by government monopolies are, in fact, natural monopolies, just as the advocates of government intervention had claimed.

However, the regulatory functions now being performed by bodies like the ACCC are not new. In the past, these functions were performed by the same statutory monopolies that provided the relevant services. From an engineering viewpoint, such integrated management has obvious advantages. In most cases, however, the accountability that arises from external regulation has yielded net benefits.

Labour market reform

As has already been noted, labour market policy under the Hawke government was an exception to the general trend towards more market-oriented policy. The Accord on Prices and Incomes strengthened the role of central wage fixation through the Arbitration Commission. Moreover, the policy deals through which the government and the Australian Council of Trade Unions reached an agreed position involving low or negative growth in real wages typically included interventionist policy initiatives, of which the most notable were Medicare and compulsory superannuation.

The centralised approach was gradually abandoned in favour of a system of enterprise bargaining, which remains the most important institutional framework for wage-setting. Subsequent reforms, such as the introduction of Australian workplace agreements (individually negotiated employment contracts) have had only a modest effect.

The effects of labour market reform, in the strict sense of changes to industrial relations policies and institutional frameworks, appear to have been modest. However, the changes in labour markets arising, directly or indirectly, from micro-economic reform have been dramatic. They include declining union membership and a reduction in the proportion of the workforce with traditional full-time jobs (35–45 hours per week), offset by growth in both part-time (mostly casual) employment and in jobs with long working hours (45+ per week). Policies that have affected labour market outcomes directly have included competitive tendering, reductions in industry assistance, and corporatisation or privatisation of government business enterprises. Indirect but equally profound effects have arisen from financial market deregulation and the resulting increase in the influence of financial markets.

Micro-economic reform and macro-economic policy

The term 'micro-economic reform' reflects a conscious contrast with the macro-economic policies that dominated economic policy in Australia from World War II to the late 1970s. However, perceptions of the relationship between micro-economic reform and macro-economic policy have changed over time.

The focus on micro-economic reform in the early 1980s reflected the failure of Keynesian stabilisation policies, and the monetarist alternative of monetary growth rules, to reverse the rise in unemployment that took place during the 1970s. Along with the rapid growth of the current account deficit following the floating of the dollar, persistent high unemployment was seen as the product of structural rigidities ensuring that policies of macro-economic stimulus would result in higher inflation rather than growth in output. Thus, micro-economic reform was initially advocated as an expansionary policy, to be combined with stimulatory fiscal policy and the wage and price restraint generated by the Accord on Prices and Incomes.

The favourable experience of the policy response to the 'Banana Republic' crisis of 1986, when a short-lived increase in interest rates succeeded in reducing the current account deficit without generating a recession, led to a new hypothesis regarding the impact of micro-economic reform. Many commentators, such as Higgins (1991), suggested that the economy had become more 'flexible' in its response to economic shocks.

Among other things, the optimistic view of the benefits of reform reflected in Higgins's assessment was used to justify the maintenance of high interest rates during 1989, as a response to inflationary pressures and current account problems. The resulting recession showed that the economy was not as flexible as had been hoped.

The recession was the longest and deepest in postwar history. The length and strength of the expansion of the 1990s can be explained, in large measure, by the severity of the preceding recession. The 10 years of expansion between 1993 and 2003 were just sufficient to reduce the rate of unemployment to 5.6 per cent, the same rate prevailing in 1989, before the onset of the recession.

Although there was some shift to fiscal stimulus during the early years of the recession, any systematic Keynesian policy was deprecated as 'pump-priming'. The government publicly adhered to a 'medium-term strategy', in which countercyclical fiscal policy was eschewed. This continued until 1992, following the replacement of Prime Minister Hawke by Paul Keating. The medium-term strategy was generally supported by advocates of micro-economic reform, who were concerned that the pace of reform might be slowed as governments sought to respond to high unemployment. The failure of the medium-term macro-economic strategy to offset the prolonged recession therefore undermined public support for micro-economic reform.

In the last few years, the history of the late 1980s has repeated itself. The experience of 1998, when Australia felt little impact from the Asian economic crisis, has been interpreted as evidence of the flexibility generated by micro-economic reform, as was the successful management of the 'Banana Republic' crisis in 1986. Parham (2002a) observes:

> Australia's growth performance since the early 1990s has been exceptional. For nine years, annual GDP growth averaged just under 4 per cent—a performance not seen since the 1960s and early 1970s. Strong growth even persisted in the midst of the 1997 Asian financial crisis and the 2001 global downturn.

> A surge in productivity growth has underpinned Australia's good performance.

There are many reasons to doubt this analysis. First, because the Reserve Bank correctly allowed the Australian dollar to depreciate against developed-country currencies, the Asian crisis did not produce a net decline in export demand. Thus, the flexibility or otherwise of the domestic economy was not tested. Exporters had to redirect exports from Asian markets to developed countries. Admittedly, this was not a miraculous feat, given that many of these exports are commodities traded in fairly well-developed markets.

The 1990s growth rate of 4 per cent per year is not remarkable for a period of economic expansion. The average growth rate in the 1980s expansion was about 4.5 per cent. Thus, the distinguishing feature of the period since the early 1990s has been the absence of a recession rather than the strength of normal economic growth.

On this point, there is no evidence for the general claim that 'flexible' free-market economies are less susceptible to macro-economic shocks than others. New Zealand, where micro-economic reform was even more radical, but where macro-economic policy was misjudged in 1997, experienced a significant downturn following the Asian crisis. More recently, claims that the US economy was recession-proof have been shown to be baseless.

The experience of the past 20 years suggests that micro-economic reform can coexist with good, bad or indifferent macro-economic policy and macro-economic outcomes. Of course, the conclusion that micro-economic reform has had little impact on macro-economic stability is not relevant to the critical question of whether, other things being equal, micro-economic reform helped to improve living standards. It is to this issue that we now turn.

The benefits and costs of micro-economic reform

Assuming that macro-economic rather than micro-economic policy is the main determinant of aggregate employment levels, two kinds of benefits might be expected from a well-designed program of micro-economic reform. First, the removal of price distortions might be expected to improve allocative efficiency. Such improvements would increase welfare but might not be captured in measures of gross domestic product. Second, micro-economic reform might generate either static or dynamic improvements in technical efficiency, which would be captured in measures of GDP and multifactor productivity.

Allocative efficiency

The most important single policy designed to improve allocative efficiency was tariff reform, accompanied by reforms to agricultural price policy. *Ex ante* projections of the results of reforms on tariffs and price policy diverged radically. Supporters of the existing policy regime predicted disaster (Warhurst 1982). Advocates of reform argued that the 'dynamic' effects of reform would lead to the growth of an innovative manufacturing sector producing elaborately transformed manufactured products for an essentially unlimited export market. At least in the medium term, it now seems clear that the outcomes of price policy reform were consistent with a standard 'static' neoclassical model. The formerly protected sector, import-competing manufacturing, contracted sharply. Growth in imports was balanced by an expansion in exports, but manufactured exports did not expand as much as was expected by many proponents of reform. Dynamic effects, if any, were modest.

Using a Harberger triangle approximation, Quiggin (1996) estimated that the removal of tariffs generated a long-run net welfare gain equal to between 1 and 3 per cent of GDP. The short-run impacts were less favourable. The period of tariff reform in Australia coincided almost exactly with the resurgence of mass unemployment throughout the developed world. In the presence of high unemployment, the adjustment costs associated with tariff reform and other policies are higher than in the case of full employment.

Moreover, because the variance of effective protection rates initially increased, welfare was actually reduced under the case-by-case approach adopted during the 1970s, as is shown in Table 5.2, which contains three sets of estimates of the welfare cost of tariffs, calculated using the data presented in Table 5.1. The first set takes account of the mean effective rate of protection but not of the variance. The second set, referred to as the low range, is derived on the assumption that elasticities of demand and supply for individual manufactured items are equal to 0.5, the same as the aggregate elasticities for manufactured items as a group. The third set, referred to as the high range, is derived from the assumption that elasticities of demand and supply for individual manufactured items are equal to 1.0, twice the aggregate elasticities for manufactured items as a group.

The first row shows a monotonic reduction in the welfare cost of protection, with a cumulative benefit equal to 1 per cent of GDP by 1991. The second and third rows show a different pattern, in which welfare costs initially rose as a result of increasing variance in protection rates. To calculate the welfare impact of the entire process, it would be necessary to evaluate the present value of a stream of losses and gains. The results of such an evaluation are ambiguous and depend on the choice of discount rates.

Table 5.2 Estimates of welfare cost of protection (% of GDP)

	Year ending June 30				
	1971	1973	1983	1988	1991
Estimated welfare cost (mean only)	1.3	0.7	0.6	0.4	0.2
Estimated welfare cost (low range)	1.9	1.1	2.5	1.7	1.1
Estimated welfare cost (high range)	2.5	1.5	4.3	3.0	1.9

Source: Author's calculations based on data from the Industry Commission

An alternative view is that the most important indicator of the distorting effect of tariffs is the peak rates on the most highly protected industries (motor vehicles, textiles, clothing and footwear). These increased in the early period of tariff reform but declined from the mid-1980s, suggesting that the period of positive net benefits began earlier than estimated by Quiggin (1996).

Productivity: miracle or myth

A consistent theme of those advocating of micro-economic reform has been the claim that reform would lead to a sustained improvement in rates of economic growth and would, therefore, lead to growth in living standards. The first such claims were made by Kasper et al. (1980). In reality, the first decade of micro-economic reform in Australia, from 1983 to 1993, was characterised by poor growth in productivity and weak economic growth. Some of this poor performance may have been the result of pre-existing problems, but the adverse impact of financial deregulation during the 1980s, and the rise of 'entrepreneurs' such as Bond, Skase and Elliott, played a substantial role.

The response of advocates of micro-economic reform to this disappointing outcome was to 'restart the clock', ignoring events before 1993 and focussing on performance during the economic expansion that began in the early 1990s.

The claim that Australia has experienced a 'productivity miracle' has been made repeatedly since the publication of Australian Bureau of Statistics (ABS) estimates suggesting that growth in multifactor productivity (MFP) reached an unprecedented annual rate of 2.4 per cent between 1993–94 and 1997–98, compared to a long-run average of around 1 per cent. Subsequent revisions and additional data yielded lower estimates of productivity growth but no corresponding reduction in rhetorical claims.

Because estimates of productivity growth rates for the 1980s were also revised downwards, the change measured between the 1980s and 1990s was still large. Hence, there was a shift in emphasis from the rate of productivity growth to the rate of acceleration from the 1980s to the 1990s. The shift in attention from the first derivative of productivity (growth) to the second derivative (acceleration) raises complex problems of interpretation that have, in general, been disregarded.

A fairly typical statement of the case may be found in Parham (2002b):

> After showing its weakest rate in the 1980s, Australia's productivity growth accelerated to new highs in the 1990s—labour productivity growth at an average 3.0 per cent a year and multifactor productivity (MFP) growth at 1.8 per cent a year.

The most serious problem with this claim is that the term 'the 1990s', which would normally be used to describe a decade, refers to a period of only six years, from 1993–94 to 1998–99, identified by the ABS as a 'productivity cycle'. In the previous cycle, which included the recession of 1989–90, the average rate of MFP growth was 0.7 per cent. In the current incomplete cycle, which began in 1999–2000, the rate has averaged 0.5 per cent.

The average productivity growth rate for the whole of the 1990s was well below that reported by Parham. Given that data are presented on a financial-year basis, there is room for debate about the appropriate starting and ending years. However it is calculated, the rate of MFP growth for the 1990s as a whole is between 1.1 and 1.5 per cent, better than the 1980s but scarcely exceptional in either historical or international terms.

Even if all the above-average MFP growth observed during the productivity cycle from 1993–94 to 1998–99 were attributed to micro-economic reform, the cumulative benefit would be equal to only 4.8 per cent of GDP, well below widely publicised official estimates for relatively minor parts of the reform program. For example, the Industry Commission (1995) estimated the benefits of 'Hilmer and related reforms' at 5.5 per cent of GDP. This estimate took no account of tariff reform, tax reform or financial deregulation.

In fact, however, at least part of the strong productivity growth of the mid-1990s must have represented the usual recovery in productivity that follows a recession. Moreover, given the poor productivity performance observed since 1998–99, it appears that some of the productivity gains realised during the 1990s were unsustainable or illusory. As is discussed below, productivity gains generated by increased work intensity are unlikely to be sustainable in the long run.

Quiggin (2001) noted that mid-1990s productivity growth was partly illusory. The treatment of the business services sector, which grew rapidly in the mid-1990s as a result of contracting out but was inappropriately excluded from the market sector, induced an upward bias in estimates of

MFP growth. The inclusion of business services in the market sector would have reduced the measured annual rate of MFP growth for the period from 1993–94 to 1998–99 by around 0.5 percentage points. It is possible that the magnitude of the distortions associated with the treatment of the business services sector has declined since 1998–99, contributing to the reduction in measured productivity growth noted above.

Work and work intensity

The salient costs of micro-economic reform have been those borne by workers in the form of increased stress and a faster pace of work. The increase in work intensity implies that effective labour input has grown more rapidly than measured hours of work, while productivity and wages per unit of effort have grown more slowly than measured productivity and hourly wages.

Although anecdotal evidence of increases in work intensity abounds, statistical evidence is limited. The Australian Workplace Industrial Relations Survey undertaken in 1995 found that a majority of employees reported increases in stress, work effort and the pace of work over the previous year, while fewer than 10 per cent reported reductions in any of these variables (Morehead et al. 1997).

Dawson, McCullough, and Baker (2002, 4) examine the increase in working hours for full-time workers and conclude:

> For many Australian workers, their families and communities, extended working hours have led to increased levels of fatigue and decreasing levels of social support. This in turn has the potential to compromise safety and the long-term health and wellbeing of workers and the organisations that employ them.

Similar evidence, based on time-use diaries, is provided by Bittman and Rice (2002).

Green and McIntosh (2001) provide evidence of increases in work intensity from the UK, which served as the model for many Australian micro-economic reforms, notably including competitive tendering and contracting. Green and Macintosh observe that the increases in work intensity are associated with higher productivity (as would be expected) and are positively correlated with exposure to competition and reductions in union density.

Further evidence may be obtained from movements in working hours for full-time workers. To the extent that an increase in working hours reflects a demand by employers for increased work effort, standard micro-economic reasoning implies that work effort per hour will also increase. Thus, we would expect to see work effort and hours of work move together in most cases. Until about 1980, average hours of work for full-time employees had declined fairly steadily for more than a century. Although there are no formal measures for work intensity, any comparison of working conditions between 1980 and, say, 1950 or 1930 indicates a reduction in work intensity. Inadequate work intensity was frequently cited as a reason for poor economic performance by advocates of micro-economic reform, such as Blandy et al. (1985).

Average hours of work for full-time employees rose between 1980 and 1994, reaching a peak of 45 hours per week, before stabilising in the late 1990s and declining slightly after 2000. Wooden and Loundes (2002) attribute the increase in working hours to an income effect arising from wage restraint during the Accord period. This seems plausible for the 1980s, but the continued increase in working hours after the end of the Accord is almost certainly due to employer demands. For example, analysis of enterprise bargaining negotiations at this time undertaken by the Australian Centre for Industrial Relations Research and Training (1999) showed that employer claims typically included items that would lead to longer and more flexible (at the employer's discretion) working hours.

Public concern about stress and the intensity of work rose steadily in line with the increase in full-time working hours. Concerns about inadequate work intensity, dominant in the 1980s, were replaced by discussion of excessive work intensity, which reached a high point in the late 1990s. The modest decline in full-time working hours that has been observed since then is consistent with the view that the increase in working hours in the early 1990s was a short-term response to the competitive pressure associated with micro-economic reform and to the increase in employer bargaining power following the recession. Since the issue of increased work intensity as a source of measured productivity growth was first raised in the mid-1990s (see, for example, Quiggin 1996), one of the central points in the debate has been the claim that increases in productivity generated by increased work intensity are unsustainable. The strong form of this claim is that work intensity will eventually return to levels more in line with workers' preferences, and that the measured productivity increases associated with increased work intensity will be reversed. The weak version is that, if work intensity stabilises at a higher level, the measured rate of productivity growth will decline in the absence of continued growth in unmeasured labour inputs. Conversely, as noted by Parham (2002a), continued growth in productivity would imply that unsustainable growth in work intensity was not a major source of measured productivity growth.[4]

Growth accounting appears to support the strong version of the unsustainability hypothesis. Full-time working hours declined after 1998–99, and it seems likely that work intensity also declined. At the same time, the rate of multifactor productivity growth fell below its long-run average.

The implications may be seen by supposing that increases in the pace of work contributed a 5 per cent increase in effective labour input during the period from 1993–94 to 1998–99 (roughly equivalent to the loss of two 10-minute tea breaks each day), and that half of this increase in work intensity has subsequently been reversed. If labour's contribution to MFP is weighted at 70 per cent, this would imply that increased work intensity contributed 3.5 percentage points of the 4.8 percentage point increase above the long-term MFP trend observed in the mid-1990s cycle, and that decreased work intensity contributed 1.75 percentage points of the 2 percentage-point shortfall in MFP growth, relative to the long-term trend, observed since 1999–2000.

Income and inequality

As Parham (2002, 22) observes, inequality in market incomes grew in both decades of the micro-economic reform period:

> The distribution of earnings among individuals became more unequal in the 1990s. However, the increase was a continuation of the growth in earnings inequality during the 1980s, rather than a step up in the 1990s.

This finding is consistent with international evidence suggesting that market-oriented reform is associated with increasing inequality of incomes. Inequality has risen substantially in the USA, the UK and New Zealand.

---

4   To be more precise, it is necessary to focus on productivity growth in excess of the long-term trend growth rate of 1 per cent.

In Australia, until the mid-1990s, growth in earnings inequality was offset, at least in part, by changes in the tax and welfare systems that were, on balance, progressive. Since 1996, a number of these changes have been reversed as a result of the extension of micro-economic reform to the tax–welfare system. The most important single changes have been the cuts in income tax rates for higher income earners introduced along with the goods and services tax, cuts in capital gains taxes and restrictions on access to welfare payments, generically referred to as 'mutual obligation'.

Consumer choice and welfare

In most, but not all, cases, micro-economic reform has been associated with an expansion of consumer choice. Although there are few well-established techniques for measurement of the benefits of consumer choice, standard arguments around revealed preference imply that more choice is always beneficial. These arguments are based on the standard model of individual consumer sovereignty. In some cases, communitarian critics of such arguments may argue that the benefits of individual choice are offset by losses of community values.

The expansion of shopping hours provides an example. From the viewpoint of individual consumers, an expansion of shopping hours is certainly beneficial. Since this benefit is not taken into account in standard measures of the output of the retail sector, this is an instance where the productivity benefits of micro-economic reform are understated. From a communitarian perspective, however, the expansion of shopping hours has eroded traditional distinctions between weekdays and weekends, and undermined a range of community activities premised on the assumption that nearly everyone will have weekends free of work.

Summary

In aggregate, micro-economic reform has been associated with a modest increase in the rate of growth of labour productivity, most of which can be attributed to increases in the pace and intensity of work. The extra growth in MFP during the productivity cycle of the 1990s, equivalent to 4.8 per cent of GDP, represents an upper bound for the aggregate benefits of micro-economic reform. A correct estimate would be closer to zero, and possibly even negative.

Rather than seeking to justify a comprehensive program of micro-economic reform in terms of largely spurious productivity benefits, or on the basis of unrelated arguments about macro-economic performance, it is preferable to assess individual reforms on a case-by-case basis. As has been argued above, some reforms have yielded positive net benefits, but others have not.

Micro-economic reform: success or disaster?

The set of policy programs advocated under the banner of 'micro-economic reform' is too complex, and the associated set of outcomes too varied, to admit any simple characterisation. Micro-economic reform has been neither the success claimed by advocates such as the Productivity Commission, nor the disaster implied by many popular critiques of 'economic rationalism'.

Taking the two decades of micro-economic reform as a whole, the aggregate impact of the reform program on the welfare of the Australian community has been small. Periods of strong growth in productivity and output, such as the mid-1990s, did little more than recover the ground lost as a result of the impact of the activities of 'entrepreneurs' in the 1980s, and the associated 'recession we had to have'. Much of the apparent productivity growth of the 1990s has been dissipated as workers find ways of winding back the increase in the hours and intensity of work extracted through the unilateral repudiation of implicit labour contracts in this period.

As with the curate's egg, the only verdict on micro-economic reform that is both brief and accurate is that it is 'good in parts'.

Bibliography

Australian Centre for Industrial Relations Research and Training. 1999. *Australia at Work: Just Managing?* Sydney: Prentice Hall.

Bailey, David. 2003. 'Is the Australian Airline Market Contestable?' (unpublished BA (Hons) thesis, University of Queensland).

Bittman, Michael and James Rice. 2002. 'The Spectre of Overwork: An Analysis of Trends Between 1974 and 1997 Using Australian Time-Use Diaries', *Labour and Industry* 12, no. 3: 5–25. doi.org/10.1080/10301763.2002.10722021.

Bishop, Steven, Peter Dodd, and Robert Officer. 1987. *Australian Takeovers: The Evidence, 1972–1985*. St Leonards, NSW: The Centre for Independent Studies.

Blandy, Richard, Peter Dawkins, Ken Gannicot, Peter Kain, Wolfgang Kasper, and Roy Kriegler. 1985. *Structured Chaos: The Process of Productivity Advance*. Oxford: Oxford University Press.

Bollard, Alan and Robert Buckle, eds. 1987. *Economic Liberalisation in New Zealand*. Wellington: Allen & Unwin in association with Port Nicholson Press.

Constantinides, George, John Donaldson, and Rajnish Mehra. 1998. 'Junior Can't Borrow: A New Perspective on the Equity Premium Puzzle'. NBER Working Paper Series no. 6617, National Bureau of Economic Research, Cambridge, MA, doi.org/10.3386/w6617.

Dawkins, Peter and Paul Kelly, eds. 2003. *Hard Heads, Soft Hearts: A New Reform Agenda for Australia*. St Leonards: Allen & Unwin.

Dawson, Drew, Kirsty McCulloch, and Angela Baker. 2002. *Extended Working Hours in Australia: Counting the Costs*. Woodville: Centre for Sleep Research, University of South Australia.

Easton, Brian. 1997. *The Commercialisation of New Zealand*. Auckland: Auckland University Press. Ebook.

Edwards, Geoff. 2003. 'The Story of Deregulation in the Dairy Industry', *Australian Journal of Agricultural and Resource Economics* 47, no. 1: 75–98. doi.org/10.1111/1467-8489.00204.

Forsyth, Peter. 1998. 'The Gains from the Liberalisation of Air Transport'. *Journal of Transport Economics and Policy* 32, no. 1: 73–92.

Fukuyama, Francis. 1992. *The End of History and the Last Man*. New York: The Free Press.

Grant, Simon and John Quiggin. 2003. 'Public Investment and the Risk Premium for Equity'. *Economica* 70, no. 277: 1–18.

Green, Francis and Steve McIntosh. 2001. 'The Intensification of Work in Europe'. *Labour Economics* 8, no. 2: 291–308. doi.org/10.1016/s0927-5371(01)00027-6.

Harberger, Arnold. 1964. 'Taxation, Resource Allocation and Welfare'. In *The Role of Direct and Indirect Taxes in the Federal Reserve System*, edited by National Bureau of Economic Research, 25–80. Princeton: Princeton University Press. doi.org/10.1515/9781400875931-003.

Hathaway, Neville. (1997). 'Privatisation and the Cost of Capital', *Agenda* 4, no. 1: 1–10.

Higgins, Chris. 1991. Opening address to the Australian Economic Policy Conference. Centre for Economic Policy Research, The Australian National University, Canberra.

Hilmer, Frederick, Mark Rayner, and Geoffrey Taperell. 1993. *National Competition Policy* (Report by the Independent Committee of Inquiry). Canberra: Australian Government Publishing Service.

Industry Commission. 1995. *The Growth and Revenue Implications of Hilmer and Related Reforms.* Canberra: Australian Government Publishing Service.

Kasper, Wolfgang, Richard Blandy, John Freebairn, Douglas Hocking, and Robert O'Neill. 1980. *Australia at the Crossroads: Our Choices to the Year 2000.* Sydney: Harcourt Brace Jovanovich.

Kocherlakota, Narayana R. 1996. 'The Equity Premium: It's Still a Puzzle'. *Journal of Economic Literature* 34, no. 1: 42–71.

Mankiw, N. Gregory. 1986. 'The Equity Premium and the Concentration of Aggregate Shocks'. *Journal of Financial Economics* 17, 211–19. doi.org/10.1016/0304-405x(86)90012-7.

Mehra, Rajnish, and Edward Prescott. 1985. 'The Equity Premium: A Puzzle'. *Journal of Monetary Economics* 15, no. 2: 145–61. doi.org/10.1016/0304-3932(85)90061-3.

Milbourne, Ross and Matthew Cumberworth. 1991. 'Australian Banking Performance in an Era of Deregulation'. *Australian Economic Papers* 30, no. 57: 171–91. doi.org/10.1111/j.1467-8454.1991.tb00538.x.

Morehead, Alison, Mairi Steele, Michael Alexander, Kerry Stephen, and Linton Duffin. 1997. *Changes at Work: The 1995 Australian Workplace Industrial Relations Survey.* Melbourne: Addison Wesley Longman Australia.

Officer, Robert. 1999. 'Privatisation of public assets'. In *Privatisation: Efficiency of Fallacy? Two Perspectives*, edited by Committee for Economic Development of Australia: 1–22.

Parham, Dean. 2002. 'Productivity Growth in Australia: Are We Enjoying a Miracle?' Presentation, Conference of the Melbourne Institute and *The Australian*, 'Towards Opportunity and Prosperity'. Melbourne, April 2002. melbourneinstitute.unimelb.edu.au/outlook/assets/2002/ParhamDean-S.pdf.

Pusey, Michael. 1991. Economic Rationalism, in *Canberra: A Nation-Building State Changes Its Mind.* Cambridge: Cambridge University Press.

Quiggin, John. 1995. 'Does Privatisation Pay?'. *The Australian Economic Review* 28, no. 2: 23–42. doi.org/10.1111/j.1467-8462.1995.tb00886.x.

Quiggin, J. 1996. *Great Expectations: Microeconomic Reform and Australia.* St Leonards, NSW: Allen & Unwin.

Quiggin, John. 1997a. 'Economic Rationalism'. *Crossings: The Bulletin of the International Australian Studies Association* 2, no. 1: 3–12.

Quiggin, John. 1997b. 'Evaluating Airline Deregulation in Australia'. *Australian Economic Review* 30, no. 1: 45–56. doi.org/10.1111/1467-8462.00004.

Quiggin, John. 2001. 'The Australian Productivity Miracle: A Sceptical View'. *Agenda* 8, no. 4: 333–48. doi.org/10.22459/ag.08.04.2001.04.

Quiggin, John. 2004. 'Looking Back on Microeconomic Reform: A Sceptical Viewpoint'. *Economic and Labour Relations Review* 15: 1–25. doi.org/10.1177/103530460401500101.

Schneider, Michael. 1998. '"Economic Rationalism", Economic Rationalists and Economists'. *Quadrant* (October): 48–53.

Sykes, Trevor. 1994. *The Bold Riders.* St Leonards: Allen & Unwin.

Walker, Robert and Betty Walker. 2000. *Privatisation: Sell Off or Sell Out?: The Australian Experience.* Sydney: ABC Books.

Warhurst, John. 1982. *Jobs or Dogma?: The Industries Assistance Commission and Australian Politics.* St Lucia: University of Queensland Press.

Weil, Philippe. 1989. 'The Equity Premium Puzzle and the Risk-Free Rate Puzzle', *Journal of Monetary Economics* 24: 401–21. doi.org/10.1016/0304-3932(89)90028-7.

Wooden, Mark and Joanne Loundes 2002. 'How Unreasonable Are Long Working Hours?'. Working Paper January 2002. Melbourne Institute of Applied Economic and Social Research, Melbourne.

6

What have we learned from the Global Financial Crisis?

First published in 2011 as Quiggin, John. 'What Have We Learned from the Global Financial Crisis?' *Australian Economic Review* 44: 355–65. doi. org/10.1111/j.1467-8462.2011.00661.x.

Introduction

The Global Financial Crisis (GFC) that brought the world's financial system to the brink of failure in September 2008 was the most significant economic event since the breakdown of the Bretton Woods system in the 1970s. Three years on, unemployment rates in the USA and the EU remain close to 10 per cent. The expenditure required to salvage the system has pushed public debt to dangerously high levels in many countries. Millions of households have faced bankruptcy or foreclosure, and millions more are still at risk.

The crisis was not anticipated by the great majority of the economics profession. Even as the financial system began to collapse in 2007 and 2008, central banks insisted that the situation was under control, and that the modest measures they had undertaken would be sufficient to maintain financial stability and economic prosperity. Admittedly, central banks are more or less obligated to maintain a confident stance in public, but there is little evidence of any private misgivings, let alone preparation for a crisis on the scale that ultimately emerged.

Meanwhile, academic macro-economists were celebrating the convergence between Real Business Cycle and New Keynesian schools (aka 'freshwater' and 'saltwater'), symbolised by the development of dynamic stochastic general equilibrium (DSGE) theory. Dynamic stochastic general equilibrium is the idea that macro-economic analysis should not be concerned with observable realities like booms and slumps, but with the theoretical consequences of optimising behaviour by perfectly rational (or almost perfectly rational) consumers, firms and workers. This convergence of the two schools fitted nicely with the 'Great Moderation', a reduction in the volatility of output and other economic variables beginning in the 1980s and first noted in the early 2000s. The results may be seen in the proceedings of a conference on the topic (Woodford 2009). I discuss the Great Moderation and DSGE theory later in this chapter.

It is of interest, then, to consider how policymakers and academic economists responded to the shock of September 2008. A large and unexpected macro-economic crisis, originating in financial markets, might be expected to yield important lessons about economic policy, economic theory and the behaviour of crucial economic variables, reflected in substantial changes in the research program of academic macro-economics, the settings of economic policy and the way in which economics is taught.

In reality, however, such changes have been modest to the point of invisibility. After a brief, though intense, embrace of Keynesian stimulus policies in the immediate aftermath of the crisis, policymakers have largely returned to the policies that produced the crisis.

Within academic economics, the effects were even more limited. While Keynesian economists such as Paul Krugman had more influence in the policy debate than before, their criticisms have had little or no impact on the practice of academic economists. Reading recent issues of the leading general journals, it would be virtually impossible to infer that the world economy had approached collapse in late 2008, that US unemployment remains near 10 per cent or that economic theory had been affected in any way by these events.

The aim of this article is to examine the lessons of the GFC, considered in terms of three different questions:

1. What should we (the economics profession) have learned from the GFC?
2. What, if anything, have we actually learned about economic theory and policy?
3. What have we learned about ourselves as a profession?

My answer to the first of these questions will be, in large measure, a summary and update of the arguments presented in Quiggin (2010). My answers to the second and third questions are thoroughly dispiriting. The lessons of the crisis have been at best half-learned, and in some cases, profoundly mistaken conclusions have been drawn.

What should we have learned?

A massive financial macro-economic crisis, largely unforeseen by the economics profession, should, at a minimum, cast doubt on the validity of the ideas that guided financial and macro-economic policy in the years leading up to the crisis. In the case of the GFC, the crisis arose in financial markets that had undergone a massive expansion as a result of economic theories and policies that arose in the 1970s, following the breakdown of an earlier consensus-supporting financial regulation and Keynesian macro-economic policies. These ideas have been variously, and mostly pejoratively, referred to as 'neoliberalism', the 'Washington Consensus' and 'economic rationalism'. In Quiggin (2010), I used the more neutral term, 'market liberalism'.

Quiggin (2010) listed five ideas central to market liberalism. Some are economic theories, some policy prescriptions, and some claims about the way the economy works. The ideas I discussed and dissected were as follows.

The Great Moderation

This is the idea that the period beginning in 1985 was one of unparalleled macro-economic stability that could be expected to endure indefinitely. Even when it was alive, this idea depended on some dubious statistical arguments and a willingness to ignore the crises that afflicted many developing economies in the 1990s. But the Great Moderation was too convenient to cavil at.

Of all the ideas I have tried to kill, this one seems most self-evidently refuted by the crisis. If double-digit unemployment rates and the deepest recession since the 1930s do not constitute an end to moderation, what does? Yet, academic advocates of the Great Moderation hypothesis, such as Coibion and Gorodnichenko (2010), have stuck to their guns, calling the financial crisis a 'transitory volatility blip'.

More importantly, central banks and other policymakers are planning a return to business as usual as soon as the crisis is past. Here, 'business as usual' means the policy package of central bank independence, inflation-targeting and reliance on interest rate adjustments that have failed so spectacularly in the crisis. Speaking at a symposium for the 50th anniversary of the Reserve Bank of Australia earlier this year (2010), the president of the European Central Bank (ECB), Jean-Claude Trichet, offered the following, startlingly complacent analysis:

> We are emerging from the uncharted waters navigated over the past few years. But as central bankers we are always faced with new episodes of turbulence in the economic and financial environment. While we grapple with how to deal with ever new challenges, we must not forget the fundamental tenets that we have learned over the past decades. Keeping inflation expectations anchored remains of paramount importance, under exceptional circumstances even more than in normal times. Our framework has been successful in this regard thus far.

The efficient markets hypothesis

This is the idea that the prices generated by financial markets represent the best possible estimate of the value of any investment. In the version most relevant to public policy, the efficient markets hypothesis states that it is impossible to outperform market valuations on the basis of any public information.

Support for the efficient markets hypothesis has always relied more on its consistency with free-market ideas in general than on clear empirical evidence. The absurdities of the dotcom bubble-and-bust of the late 1990s ought to have killed the notion. However, given the explosive growth and massive profitability of the financial sector in the early 2000s, the hypothesis was too convenient to give up. Some advocates developed elaborate theories to show that the billion-dollar values placed on companies delivering dog food over the internet were actually rational. Others simply treated the dotcom bubble as the exception that proves the rule.

Either way, the lesson was the same: governments should leave financial markets to work their magic without interference. That lesson was followed with undiminished faith until it came to the edge of destroying the global economy in late 2008.

Even now, however, when the efficient financial markets hypothesis should be discredited once and for all, and when few are willing to advocate it publicly, it lives on in zombie form. This is most evident in the attention paid to rating agencies and bond markets in the discussion of the so-called 'sovereign debt crisis' in Europe, despite the fact that it was the failure of these very institutions, and the speculative bubble they helped to generate, that created the crisis in the first place.

Dynamic stochastic general equilibrium

The DSGE macro arose out of the breakdown of the economic synthesis that informed public policy in the decades after World War II, which combined Keynesian macro-economics with neoclassical micro-economics. In the wake of the stagflation of the 1970s, critics of Keynes, such as Lucas (1980), argued that macro-economic analysis of employment and inflation must instead be derived from, and therefore be consistent with, neoclassical micro-economic foundations.

The result was a thing of intellectual beauty, compared by the IMF's Chief Economist, Olivier Blanchard (2008), to a haiku. By adding just the right twists to the model, it was possible to represent booms and recessions, at least on the modest scale that prevailed during the Great Moderation. Moreover, modestly Keynesian twists yielded support for the dominant monetary policy framework, based on Taylor rules (Taylor 1993). But, when the crisis came, all this sophistication proved useless. It was not just that DSGE models failed to predict the crisis; they also contributed nothing to the discussion of policy responses, which has all been conducted with reference to simple Keynesian and classical models that can be described by the kinds of graphs found in introductory textbooks.

Krugman (2009) has written that the profession has mistaken beauty for truth, a sentiment shared by many others. We need macro-economic analysis that is more realistic, even if it is less rigorous. That said, the supertanker of an academic research agenda is hard to turn, and the DSGE approach has steamed on, unaffected by its failure in practice. As of September 2011, Google Scholar lists more than 5,000 articles on DSGE macro-economics published since 2009, and many more are on the way.

The trickle-down hypothesis

The trickle-down hypothesis holds that policies that benefit the wealthy will ultimately help everybody. Unlike some of the zombie ideas discussed here, trickle-down economics has long been with us. The term itself seems to have been coined by cowboy performer Will Rogers (1932), who observed Herbert Hoover's tax cuts of 1928: 'The money was all appropriated for the top in the hopes that it would trickle down to the needy. [...] Mr Hoover ... dident [*sic*] know that money trickled up' (Rogers, 1932).

Trickle-down economics was conclusively refuted by the experience of the postwar economic golden age. During this 'great compression', massive reductions in inequality brought about by strong unions and progressive taxes co-existed with full employment and sustained economic growth.

Whatever the evidence, an idea as convenient to the rich and powerful as trickle-down economics cannot be kept down for long. As inequality grew in the 1980s, supply-siders and Chicago school economists promised that, sooner or later, everyone would benefit. This idea gained more support during the triumphalist years of the 1990s, when, for the only time since the breakdown of Keynesianism in the 1970s, the benefits of growth were widely spread, and when stock-market booms promised to make everyone rich.

The GFC marks the end of an economic era and provides us with a position to survey how the benefits of economic growth have been shared since the 1970s. The answers are striking. Most of the benefits of US economic growth went to those in the top percentile of the income distribution. By 2007, just one out of 100 Americans received nearly one-quarter of all personal income, more than the bottom 50 per cent of households put together (Saez 2009).

The rising tide of wealth has conspicuously failed to lift all boats. Median household income has declined in the USA over the last decade and has been stagnant since the 1970s. Wages for men with high-school education have fallen substantially over the same period.

Whatever the facts, there will always be plenty of advocates for policies that favour the rich. Sowell (2010, 283) provides a fine example, observing:

> If mobility is defined as being free to move, then we can all have the same mobility, even if some end up moving faster than others and some of the others do not move at all.

Translating to the real world, Sowell is saying that if we observe one set of children born into a wealthy family, with parents willing and able to provide high-quality schooling and 'legacy' admission to the Ivy League universities they attended, and another family whose parents struggled to put food on the table, we should not be concerned that members of the first group almost invariably do better. After all, some people from very disadvantaged backgrounds achieve success and there is no law preventing the rest from doing so.

Contrary to the cherished beliefs of most Americans, the USA has less social mobility than any other developed country. Haskins and Sawhill (2009) show that 42 per cent of American men with fathers in the bottom fifth of the income distribution remain there, as compared to Denmark (25 per cent), Sweden (26 per cent), Finland (28 per cent), Norway (28 per cent) and the UK (30 per cent). The American dream is fast becoming a myth.

Privatisation

This is the idea that nearly any function now undertaken by government could be done better by private firms. The boundaries between the private and public sectors have always shifted back and forth, but the general tendency since the late 19th century has been for the role of the state to expand in order to correct the limitations and failures of market outcomes. Beginning with Margaret Thatcher's government in 1980s Britain, there was a concerted global attempt to reverse this process. The theoretical basis for privatisation rested on the efficient markets hypothesis, according to which private markets would always yield better investment decisions and more efficient operations than public-sector planners.

The political imperative derived from the 'fiscal crisis of the state' arose when the growing commitments of the welfare state ran into the end of the sustained economic growth on which it was premised. The crisis manifested itself in the 'tax revolts' of the 1970s and 1980s, such as California's Proposition 13, the ultimate source of the state's current crisis.

Even in its heyday, privatisation failed to deliver on its promises. Public enterprises were sold at prices that failed to recompense governments for their loss of earnings. Rather than introducing a new era of competition, privatisation commonly replaced public monopolies with private monopolies, which have sought all kinds of regulatory arbitrage to maximise their profits. Australia's Macquarie Bank, which specialises in such monopoly assets and is known as the 'millionaires' factory', has shown particular skill in jacking up prices and charges in ways not anticipated by governments undertaking privatisation.

Privatisation has failed even more spectacularly in the 21st century. A series of high-profile privatisations, including those of Air New Zealand and Railtrack in Britain, were reversed. Then, in the chaos of the GFC, giants like General Motors and American Insurance Group sought the protection of government ownership.

Sensible proponents of the mixed economy have never argued that privatisation should be opposed in all cases. As circumstances change, government involvement in some areas of the economy becomes more desirable, in others less so. However, the idea that change should always be in the direction of greater private ownership deserves to be consigned to the graveyard of dead ideas.

What have we learned?

The ideas that drove the crisis are not dead. They continue to roam the landscape in undead, or zombie, form. Nevertheless, some lessons have been learned, or at least half-learned. Among these are the following.

The business cycle is with us forever

The Great Moderation was far from the first version of the claim that the business cycle had been tamed once and for all. Keynesians made the same claim in the 1960s, the strongest version being the claim (commonly attributed to Walter Heller) that the instruments of fiscal and monetary policy could be used to 'fine-tune' macro-economic performance. Shiller (2000) points to earlier examples.

Belief in the Great Moderation, along with the ideology of neoliberalism, led most economic policymakers to ignore, or view benignly, economic imbalances that would previously have created great alarm. This was most obvious in relation to large trade imbalances, which were seen by advocates of the 'consenting adults' hypothesis as inherently benign, even at levels well outside previous experience, such as those that characterised the so-called Icelandic miracle. As I observed at the time (Quiggin 2006):

Iceland seems like an ideal, if somewhat extreme, test case for this viewpoint. The government has maintained consistent budget surpluses, and pursued liberal economic policies, just as the consenting adults view suggests. On the other hand, even allowing for the volatility associated with a small economy, Iceland's current account deficits are far beyond the level which should, on traditional views, lead inevitably to an economic crisis.

The subsequent collapse of the Icelandic financial sector, and with it the entire economy, showed that the traditional view was correct.

Financial markets are valuable but dangerous

The dangers of unfettered financial markets have been evident ever since the early 18th century, which saw the South Sea Bubble in Britain and the Mississippi bubble in France. The lessons of these early bubbles have been forgotten and relearned repeatedly over subsequent centuries. Economists as diverse as Fisher, Keynes and Hayek produced analyses of financial market instability. Nevertheless, every new boom produced a new crop of theorists eager to proclaim that 'this time is different' (Reinhart and Rogoff 2009).

No episode of forgetting was as complete and consistent as that of the 1990s and early 2000s. Not only was the standard claim that 'this time is different' repeated with new vigour, but an intellectual cottage industry arose to explain away previous disasters such as the Dutch tulip mania (Garber 2001) and even the Great Depression (Cole and Ohanian 2004). The efficient markets hypothesis, in its various forms, enabled defenders of financial markets to shift between ultra-strong claims, on the one hand, that financial markets provide the best possible guide to investment and asset value, and ultra-weak fallback positions on the other, such as the observation that it is impossible for everyone to bet successfully against the market.

The GFC has shattered these beliefs, but progress towards a better understanding of financial markets has been very limited. The result has been a set of contradictory policies. On the one hand, the obvious failures of the light-handed systems of regulation epitomised by the Basel II framework[1] have produced a series of initiatives at the national and global

---

1   The Basel Committee on Banking Regulations, headquartered at the Bank for International Settlements in Basel, was established to enhance financial stability by improving the quality of banking supervision worldwide. The Committee has established a series of international standards for bank regulation, most notably its landmark publications of the accords on capital adequacy, commonly known as Basel I, Basel II and, most recently, Basel III. See www.bis.org/bcbs/history.htm.

level designed to prevent a repetition of these failures. Most notably, the Basel III framework has tightened up capital requirements across the board. On the other hand, moves towards more fundamental reform, aimed at reducing the size and cost of the financial system, have gone nowhere. On the contrary, the main concern of policymakers has been to restore pre-crisis 'normality' as rapidly as possible.

We are all Keynesians in a crisis

Finally, it seems that we have learned that, whatever the theoretical case for nonintervention, no government or central bank will permit a complete economic collapse of the type that threatened national economies in late 2008. Unlike the conditions of 'ordinary' recession governments are willing to tolerate at present, such a collapse threatens everyone, not merely the unemployed.

The initial reaction to the crisis was a return to Keynesian fiscal stimulus, even by governments like that of Germany, where Keynesianism has had little support. Broadly speaking, the experience of the crisis supported the Keynesian view. Countries that adopted a large discretionary fiscal stimulus, notably, including China and Australia, performed much better than those that did not.

Unfortunately, it is difficult to obtain a clean experiment in fiscal policy. Discretionary fiscal policy is designed to be countercyclical, and automatic stabilisers are countercyclical by definition, meaning that fiscal stimulus will be positively correlated, over time, with recessions. Deriving lessons from comparative performance in the GFC raises a different kind of problem. The strongest discretionary fiscal stimulus was undertaken in countries such as China and Australia, where the shock was entirely external and where policymakers had some warning of its arrival. The good outcomes experienced in these countries might be, and have been attributed to, the absence of a domestic shock. A rather less convincing counterargument, often heard in the Australian debate, is that our relatively good performance depended on strong demand from China rather than on policies of fiscal stimulus. Since China adopted the same policies, this appears to be a claim that Keynesianism works, but only in China.

More importantly, perhaps, the fiscal stimulus policy adopted by the Obama Administration in the USA was half-hearted and poorly targeted, and it became confused, at least in the minds of the public, with the equally poorly designed bailout of the US banking system undertaken in the dying days of the Bush Administration. As a result, the US fiscal stimulus has been widely regarded as a failure.

Unfortunately, therefore, the Keynesian lessons were only half-learned. As soon as the immediate crisis was past, there was a resurgence of anti-Keynesian and, to a large extent, pre-Keynesian thinking. However, the picture is not entirely bleak. In Australia, the Treasury has adopted a consistently Keynesian analysis. International bodies such as the IMF have also tended to look at the evidence more broadly and to support an expansionary stance in both fiscal and monetary policy. Nevertheless, the dominant trend in policy has been towards a rapid reversal of Keynesian stimulus.

The wrong lesson: austerity

As the crisis has continued, the main focus of attention has turned away from the evident failure of financial markets and towards the alleged failings of governments. The underlying ideas can be seen as a revival of the 'Treasury view' of the 1920s.

The Treasury view embodies two key elements. In fiscal policy, the Treasury view embodies a predominant—indeed, near-exclusive—focus on keeping faith with bondholders, rejecting not only default but any tolerance of inflation as a way of sharing the burden of unsound debt. This position is intertwined with a contractionist macro-economic analysis, in which cuts in budget deficits are supposed to promote 'business confidence', particularly if they are achieved through reductions in expenditure.

Austerity policies have been adopted even where there is no immediate crisis in public debt, as in the UK and the USA, but the problem has been sharpest in Europe. In the process of bailing out the financial systems and responding to the sharp downturn in economic activity, European governments guaranteed private debt and took on substantial debts of their own. For many peripheral countries, such as Portugal, Ireland, Greece and Spain, these debts have proved unsustainable. Now, the bondholders are demanding that full repayment of their claims should be ensured by the adoption of 'austerity' measures that are virtually certain to produce a new recession if implemented as planned.

Over the last year and a half, Europe has taken a set of stop-gap measures aimed at protecting its weaker economies against pressures from bond markets. European states have sought to propitiate bond markets through enforcing economic austerity and ruthlessly cutting spending. There is considerable pressure, notably from the German government and the ECB, to institutionalise austerity.

Institutionalised austerity will badly damage European economies in the short term. However, its long-term consequences will be much, much worse. Even if these measures somehow calm bond markets, they will utterly destroy the EU's remaining political legitimacy. European politicians worry about the economic consequences of failure. They should be far more worried about the political consequences. The system they are drifting towards is a thinly disguised version of the gold standard that wreaked havoc in the 1920s and will have the same toxic political fallout.

The situation in the USA is equally dire. At the state and local level, the combination of declining revenues and balanced-budget requirements has necessitated large-scale reductions in both employment and services. This, in turn, has contributed to the length and depth of the US recession.

At the federal level, the same pattern is now emerging. After the initial round of fiscal stimulus in 2009, the Obama Administration took the view that the economy would recover without additional intervention. By the time the falsehood of that view became clear, the 2010 elections had produced a Republican majority in the House of Representatives.

The new Congress was resolutely opposed to any further fiscal stimulus. Moreover, by threatening to enforce a default on US government debt, the Republicans were able to negotiate a policy package involving large-scale expenditure cuts. The efforts of the Obama Administration to negotiate a 'grand bargain', in which these and further cuts would be combined with modest increases in tax revenue, cemented a consensus on the need for immediate adoption of austerity policies, despite weak economic growth and a continuing decline in the US employment–population ratio.

Experience under austerity policies has confirmed the validity of the Keynesian analysis. There has been no general recovery, and performance has been particularly disappointing in the USA and UK, where austerity measures have been chosen, even in the absence of an immediate budgetary crisis.

What have we learned about ourselves?

The experience of the crisis suggests some unflattering lessons about the economics profession, taken broadly to include academic economists, policymakers, central bankers and commentators. The collapse of the Great Moderation, and the near-collapse of the global financial system, provided the profession with an opportunity and, indeed, an urgent imperative for a fundamental reconsideration of ideas that had been taken for granted for 30 years or more.

Unfortunately, like the Bourbon monarchs returning after the fall of Napoleon, we have, for the most part, learned nothing and forgotten nothing. Across a broad spectrum, the economics profession has sought the fastest possible return to pre-crisis normalcy, ignoring the obvious evidence that it was precisely the 'normal' assumptions of neoliberalism that produced the crisis.

The problems are most evident in the behaviour of central banks, which remain the dominant force in the determination of macro-economic policy. In the years leading up to the crisis, central bankers were congratulating themselves on the creation of an inflation-targeting system that had finally hit both the explicit target of low and stable inflation and the implicit target of steady and stable growth in real output (that is, the Great Moderation).

It is a simple matter of record that the policies adopted by central banks during the Great Moderation did not prevent its catastrophic collapse. More seriously, there is a good deal of evidence to suggest that long periods of low and stable inflation are actually conducive to asset price bubbles such as those that led to the GFC.

At a minimum, this experience should have suggested a rethinking of the system of inflation targeting. Even assuming a continuation of inflation targeting, the current debt deflation clearly calls for a higher inflation target, at least in the short run. Looking beyond this purely technical adjustment, the use of alternative targets, such as the price level or nominal income, might help to avoid the potential for deflationary liquidity traps inherent in the inflation-targeting approach.

A more serious response to the crisis would be the recognition that a single instrument, such as a short-term interest rate, is insufficient when the central bank must not only achieve a balance between inflation and output growth, as proposed by the Taylor rule, but must also maintain the systemic stability of the financial system. The latter requirement suggests the need for a reconsideration of the separation between monetary policy and prudential regulation that was a central feature of the reforms of the neoliberalism era.

The general policy community, including economic commentators, think tanks and policymakers, has done little better. The fact that Australia escaped the GFC largely unscathed has meant that economic commentators have felt free to ignore it. As Terry McCrann (2009, 21) wrote in dismissing proposals for an inquiry into the financial system: 'Not many dead or even injured in Australia. From any systemic fault, that's to say.'

As the GFC has faded further into memory, attention has returned to the tired micro-economic reform agenda of the 1980s. Misleading statistics on productivity have been used to argue the need for a new round of reform. It would be far more useful to focus attention on the macro-economic risks that still face us, most notably in the event of a slump, or even a slowdown, in China's economic growth.

Turning to the academic economics profession, it would be unfair to say that economists have ignored the evidence of the financial crisis. On the contrary, vast numbers of papers are now being written to incorporate financial shocks into econometric and macro-economic models. But there is no suggestion, as there was in both the 1930s and the 1970s, that the GFC necessitates any reassessment of the ideas that have dominated economic thinking since the 1970s or any significant change in the way in which economics is done.

In terms of the way in which economics is done, the selection of articles published in economics journals today is almost indistinguishable from that of, say, 2007. The central focus is on incremental contributions on topics of fashionable interest. The aesthetic criteria on which articles are judged (focussed primarily on theoretical rigour) means that there is no place in the journals for the reconsideration of fundamental issues. Almost the only exception is the publication of presidential addresses and the like, where the most firmly established members of the profession are given some licence to speculate.

As far as content is concerned, the majority of economic research deals with issues that are, while not necessarily irrelevant to policy concerns, far removed from the most pressing issues of the day. This has probably always been true to some extent,[2] and the need for external funding for most research has only exacerbated the problem.

An obvious difference between the GFC and the crises of the 1930s and 1970s is the absence, at least so far, of a well-developed alternative to the dominant model rendered problematic by the crisis. Keynes (1936) offered an alternative to the orthodoxy of classical and neoclassical economics, which maintained the impossibility of sustained high unemployment, except as the product of distortions in the labour market. Keynes also offered a solution—the use of fiscal policy to stabilise aggregate demand—and this policy was adopted, with great success, after 1945.

When Keynesian economics itself ran into difficulties, beginning in the late 1960s, the monetarism of Milton Friedman (1968) presented itself as an alternative. No such alternative is yet available to us. Our position is most analogous to that faced by economists in the early years of the Great Depression before the emergence of the Keynesian alternative to the dominant Treasury view. It is, perhaps, too much to hope for the emergence of a new Keynes or Friedman who can present a comprehensive analysis of the failures of the current model and point the way forward to a new one.

Rather, we must look for a synthesis, recovering the central insights of the Keynesian revolution while retaining what was valuable in Friedman's counterrevolution, and incorporating the insights of more recent work on behavioural economics. That is a demanding research program, and it is far from clear where it will lead. All the more reason, then, for the profession to make a start along these lines—if necessary, at the expense of established research programs whose inadequacies have been shown up by the GFC.

---

2   Many years ago, I was struck by reading a survey of the articles published in economic journals during the Great Depression, which found that only a small proportion addressed the problems of unemployment, macro-economic policy and other issues related to the economic crisis that had engulfed the world. Unfortunately, I did not record the reference and have never again been able to locate this article. Nevertheless, it had a significant impact on my own research priorities.

Less hubris?

The central theme of Quiggin (2010), reflected in the title *Zombie Economics*, was that, although the ideas and policies central to neoliberalism[3] had been refuted by events, they nonetheless remain influential. Less than a year since the book appeared, the resurgence of these zombie ideas is now almost complete.

Despite being spectacularly discredited by the GFC, the ideas of neoliberalism continue to guide the thinking of many, if not most, policymakers and commentators. In part, that is because these ideas are useful to rich and powerful interest groups. In part, it reflects the inherent tenacity of intellectual commitments. Most importantly, though, the survival of these zombie ideas reflects the absence of a well-developed alternative. Economics must take new directions in the 21st century if we are to avoid a repetition of the recent crisis.

Most obviously, there needs to be a shift from rigour to relevance. The prevailing emphasis on mathematical and logical rigour has given economics an internal consistency that is missing in other social sciences. However, there is little value in being consistently wrong.

Similarly, there needs to be a shift from efficiency to equity. Three decades of neoliberals pushing policies based on ideas of efficiency, and claims about the efficiency of financial markets, have not produced much in the way of improved economic performance, but they have led to drastic increases in inequality, particularly in the English-speaking world. Economists need to return their attention to policies that will generate a more equitable distribution of income.

Finally, with the collapse of yet another economic 'new era', it is time for the economics profession to display more humility and less hubris. More than two centuries after Adam Smith, economists have to admit the force of Socrates's observation that: 'The wisest man is he who knows that he knows nothing.'

---

3   I used the term 'market liberalism'.

Bibliography

Blanchard, Olivier. 2008. 'The state of macro'. Working Paper no. 14259, National Bureau of Economic Research, Cambridge, MA.

Coibion, Olivier, and Yuriy Gorodnichenko. 2010. 'Does the Great Recession Really Mean the End of the Great Moderation?'. Centre for Economic and Policy Research. cepr.org/voxeu/columns/does-great-recession-really-mean-end-great-moderation.

Cole, Harold, and Lee Ohanian. 2004. 'New Deal Policies and the Persistence of the Great Depression: A General Equilibrium Analysis'. *Journal of Political Economy* 112: 779–816. doi.org/10.1086/421169.

Friedman, Milton. 1968. 'The Role of Monetary Policy'. *American Economic Review* 58: 1–17.

Garber, Peter. 2001. *Famous First Bubbles: The Fundamentals of Early Manias*, Cambridge: MIT Press.

Haskins, Ron, and Isabel Sawhill. 2009. *Creating an Opportunity Society*. Washington, DC: Brookings Institution Press.

Keynes, John Maynard. 1936. *The General Theory of Employment, Interest and Money*. London: MacMillan.

Krugman, Paul. 2009. 'How Did Economists Get It So Wrong?'. *New York Times*, 2 September 2009. www.nytimes.com/2009/09/06/magazine/06Economic-t.html.

Lucas, Robert. 1980. 'Methods and Problems in Business Cycle Theory'. *Journal of Money, Credit and Banking* 12, no. 4. Part 2: Rational Expectations: 696–715.

McCrann, Terry. 2009. 'The Loan Rangers' Ride', *Herald Sun*, 9 July 2009: 21.

Quiggin, John. 2006. 'Taking Iceland's Hot Tip'. *Australian Financial Review*, 22 June 2006.

Quiggin, John. 2010. *Zombie Economics: How Dead Ideas Still Walk Among Us*. Princeton: Princeton University Press.

Quiggin, John. 2011. 'What Have We Learned from the Global Financial Crisis?'. *Australian Economic Review* 44: 355–65. doi.org/10.1111/j.1467-8462.2011.00661.x.

Reinhart, Carmen, and Kenneth Rogoff. 2009. *This Time Is Different: Eight Centuries of Financial Folly*. Princeton: Princeton University Press.

Rogers, Will. 1932. 'And Here's How It All Happened'. *The Tulsa Daily World*, 5 December 1932. Quoted in Wikiquotes. 'Will Rogers', last modified 1 August 2022. en.wikiquote.org/wiki/Will_Rogers.

Saez, Emanuel. 2009. 'Striking It Richer: The Evolution of Top Incomes in the United States (Update with 2007 Estimates).' Unpublished paper, Department of Economics, University of California, Berkeley.

Shiller, Robert. 2000. *Irrational Exuberance*. Princeton: Princeton University Press.

Sowell, Thomas. 2010. *Intellectuals and Society*. New York: Basic Books.

Taylor, John. 1993. 'Discretion Versus Policy Rules in Practice'. *Carnegie-Rochester Conference Series on Public Policy* 39: 195–214. doi.org/10.1016/0167-2231 (93)90009-l.

Trichet, Jean-Claude. 2010. 'Commentary on "Fifty Years of Monetary Policy: What Have We Learned?" by Adam Cagliarini, Christopher Kent and Glenn Stevens'. *BIS Review* 14.www.bis.org/review/r100211a.pdf.

Woodford, Michael. 2009. 'Convergence in macroeconomics: Elements of the New Synthesis'. *American Economic Journal: Macroeconomics* 1, no. 1: 267–79. doi.org/10.1257/mac.1.1.267.

7

The lost golden age of productivity growth?

First published in 2011 as Quiggin, John. *The Lost Golden Age of Productivity Growth?* Sydney: Reserve Bank of Australia, 367–77.

Productivity was both the Holy Grail and the founding myth of economic reform in Australia. Established in 1989 at the peak of enthusiasm for micro-economic reform,[1] the government authority responsible for promoting reform is the Productivity Commission. From the 1980s to the Global Financial Crisis (GFC) of 2008 and beyond, no discussion of Australian economic conditions was complete without an invocation of the need for Australians to 'increase their productivity', a phrase that rapidly became recognised as code for 'work harder for less pay'.[2]

The founding myth of micro-economic reform was the claim that the nation's economy experienced a surge in productivity in the mid-1990s following the round of reforms that began with the floating of the Australian dollar in 1983.[3] The putative surge was particularly welcomed by advocates of micro-economic reform, given that the decade following the float was

---

1   Treasurer Paul Keating, the politician primarily responsible for micro-economic reform, declared at the time: 'I guarantee if you walk into any pet shop in Australia, the resident galah will be talking about micro-economic policy'.
2   A striking illustration of this took place in 2011, when then Treasury Secretary Martin Parkinson gave a speech on productivity. Although Parkinson did not mention work intensity, his speech was reported on by two different news organisations under the headline 'Australians must work harder'.
3   The Whitlam government's tariff reforms, and its replacement of the old Tariff Board with the Industries Assistance Commission, the precursor of the Productivity Commission, are generally seen as a false start and were largely reversed by subsequent protectionist measures.

characterised by relatively weak productivity growth, macro-economic performance that began well but ended in the deep recession of 1989–91, and the prolonged period of high unemployment that followed.

The case for the surge was based on estimates of multifactor productivity (MFP) calculated by the Australian Bureau of Statistics (ABS). The striking finding of the ABS estimates was that the rate of MFP growth had accelerated to more than 2 per cent per year. This was seen as proof that micro-economic reform was working, and that the economy had entered a new era of sustained productivity growth.

At the time, I argued that the supposed surge in productivity reflected an increase in work intensity (Quiggin 2000), and predicted that:

> [m]uch of the apparent productivity growth of the 1990s is likely to dissipate as workers find ways of winding back the increase in the hours and intensity of work extracted through the unilateral repudiation of implicit labour contracts in this period. (Quiggin 2004, 23)

This prediction was borne out. The ABS estimate of quality-adjusted MFP declined over the period 2003–04 to 2007–08. For the entire period since 1998–99, the average annual rate of MFP growth has been 0.08 per cent, statistically indistinguishable from zero. Despite the accuracy of the predictions it generated, the view that measured changes in MFP growth rates are driven by changes in work intensity was ignored in the broader policy discussion around micro-economic reform.

The idea that the productivity miracle of the 1990s might instead have been a mirage is almost never raised. Instead, two contradictory accounts have emerged. Although they share an unquestioning acceptance of the measured productivity surge of the 1990s, they differ in their accounts of the 2000s.

The dominant view among economists is one of a 'lost golden age'. The disappearance of measured productivity growth in the 2000s is taken as a reflection of a real deterioration in economic performance, which is attributed to a slowdown or reversal of the process of micro-economic reform. In this analysis, the favourable terms of trade associated with globally high prices for minerals and strong demand from China are seen as having cushioned Australians from the harsh realities of the need for continued productivity growth.

An alternative view is that while the measured productivity surge of the 1990s was real, the reversal in measured productivity growth in the early 2000s was primarily attributable to special factors and measurement problems. This view was maintained vigorously by the Productivity Commission during the early 2000s and is maintained to some extent in its ongoing discussions of this issue.

The conventional wisdom implicit in most discussions of the Australian economy is a somewhat incoherent mixture of these two ideas. On the one hand, in discussions of micro-economic issues, the lost golden-age view dominates. It is reflected in calls for a new round of micro-economic reform. On the other hand, in discussions of Australia's strong macro-economic performance during the Global Financial Crisis (GFC), a considerable share of credit is commonly attributed to the flexibility derived from micro-economic reform.

Productivity: a problematic concept

Confusion about productivity growth is largely due to the problematic nature of productivity as a concept. At first sight, productivity seems like a simple generalisation of straightforward concepts such as crop yield (the output of a given crop per unit of land) or the number of units of a given good that a worker can produce in an hour. In national accounting, the single good in these examples is replaced by an aggregate output index such as gross domestic product (GDP). More importantly, aggregate measures of both labour and capital[4] are taken into account as inputs to production.

The starting point for the theory of productivity is the growth accounting framework developed by Solow (1956). In the standard model, the technology at time t is given by:

$Y(t) = AK(t)^{\alpha} L(t)^{-\alpha}$

$\log(Y(t)) = \alpha \log (K(t)) + (1 - \alpha) \log (L(t)) + \log(A(t))$

---

4   The question of whether, and how, heterogeneous items of equipment could be aggregated into a single capital input was the subject of the famous Cambridge capital controversy in the mid-20th century. Felipe and Fisher (2003) provide a summary of the issues.

in which Y is output, K is capital input and L is (quality-adjusted) labour. The weighted average $K(t)^{\alpha} L(t)^{1-\alpha}$ is an aggregate measure of labour and capital inputs. The third term, A, is the ratio of output to this aggregate and is therefore referred to as MFP. Since MFP appears as a residual in econometric estimates of growth equations, it is often called the Solow residual.

Within this model increases in output per worker can be caused by:

- an increase in capital stock per worker (capital deepening).
- an increase in the quality of labour input (education/experience).
- an increase in effort per worker.
- an increase in MFP.

Except in the context of debates over micro-economic reform, the Solow residual is normally taken to reflect technological change or, more precisely, 'disembodied' technical change. To the extent that technological change takes the form of more powerful and efficient capital equipment, it should be represented by an increase in the capital stock—that is, by capital deepening.

When Solow models were first estimated in the 1950s, the residual was found to be very large. However, the residual—that is, the estimated rate of MFP growth—has fallen over time. In part, this is because early estimates failed to take account of labour quality. More significantly, the mid-20th century was a period of steady technological progress for the economy as a whole. By contrast, recent decades have seen rapid technological change in information and communications technology (ICT), along with relative stagnation elsewhere. Improvements in ICT are embodied in faster, more powerful and cheaper devices; they, therefore, take the form of capital deepening. This means that, in an economy in which technological progress is embodied in capital equipment and the effects of education on human capital are properly taken into account, these two factors should fully explain observed growth in output. That is, the rate of MFP growth should be zero.

The central claim of micro-economic reform is that the standard growth model fails to account for inefficiencies caused by bad public policy. These inefficiencies mean that the actual level of output is below the potential level given by the above equations. If reforms remove these inefficiencies, productivity growth will be greater than can be accounted for by technological change alone. Particularly in the case in which all technological change is embodied, so that the underlying rate of MFP growth is zero, micro-economic reform is the sole source of MFP growth. The converse is also true. If the effect of public policy is to reduce technical efficiency, this will make a negative contribution to MFP growth.

Problems with the growth accounting framework

Standard productivity measures fail to take account of the intensity with which capital and labour are used. To understand this problem, it is useful to consider the ways in which sustainable improvements in living standards can be generated. The most important improvement, by far, is technological progress—the introduction and adoption of technological innovations such as new products and improved production technologies. There is a much-cited statement of Krugman's (1997, 11) that:

> productivity is not everything, but in the long run it is almost everything. A country's ability to improve its standard of living over time depends almost entirely on its ability to raise its output per worker.

His assertion would be equally valid if the word 'productivity' were replaced by 'technological progress'.

For a small country like Australia, the rate of technological innovation is essentially exogenous. Furthermore, to the extent that innovation takes the form of a reduction in the cost of imported ICT equipment, it is measured as capital deepening. National policies can affect the rate of adoption of new technologies. In particular, new technologies are usually more skill-intensive and knowledge-intensive than old technologies, meaning that rapid adoption of new technologies is feasible only with a skilled and educated workforce. Hence, investment in human capital can yield high returns.

The second potential source of improvement in living standards is a more efficient use of endowments of capital and labour. This may be achieved either as a result of good macro-economic outcomes (full or optimal employment of labour and capital) or good micro-economic outcomes (output closer to the technological frontier for individual enterprises and industries).

Productivity measures, at least conceptually, exclude benefits arising from good macro-economic outcomes but include the benefits of good micro-economic outcomes. In practice, however, the two are intertwined. Capital utilisation generally declines during recessions, while capital may be operated to yield unsustainably high service flows during booms. Standard productivity measures are based on the assumption that capital services are proportional to the capital stock. As the Organisation for Economic Co-operation and Development (OECD) (2001, Section 5.6) observes, attempts to include proxies for capital utilisation have proved problematic.

Measurement of labour input is even more problematic. On the one hand, labour hoarding during recessions tends to reduce productivity, producing a pro-cyclical pattern of labour productivity. On the other hand, increased employment during expansions results in the recruitment of more marginal workers, producing anti-cyclical productivity. Historically, the first of these tendencies has predominated, producing pro-cyclical productivity. But, as labour hoarding has declined, notably in the USA, productivity has become more anti-cyclical.

The use of a measure designed to include the benefits of good micro-economic outcomes and to exclude the benefits of good macro-economics is consistent with the thinking that has dominated Australian policy discussions since the 1980s, but it is deeply misleading. The primary reason for Australia's relatively strong growth in income per person since the early 1990s is the fact that, through a combination of good luck and good policy decisions, we have not experienced a recession.

MFP estimates from the ABS

The ABS began reporting estimates of MFP growth in the 1990s, calculated back to the 1960s. The initial estimates of MFP growth for the mid-1990s were in excess of 2 per cent per year, a very high rate. These were subsequently revised downwards to 1.6 per cent. Unfortunately, the ABS currently reports MFP only for the period beginning 1998–99, although older estimates are given by Campbell and Withers (2017).

The issue is further clouded by the fact that the ABS reports MFP estimates in productivity cycles that typically last about five years. The productivity cycle is a data-driven concept with no explicit theoretical basis. Productivity cycles do not necessarily correspond to business cycles, and productivity cycles in different industries are largely uncorrelated. Nevertheless, as I have shown elsewhere for the Australian economy as a whole, the MFP cycles reported by the ABS largely reflected the phases of the business cycle (Quiggin 2000). A typical business cycle contained two productivity cycles, with productivity growth stronger in the cycle corresponding to the expansion phase and weaker in the cycle corresponding to the contraction phase (Dolman, Lu, and Rahman 2006).

The productivity cycle plays a crucial role in the myth of the 1990s productivity surge, since it allows the years of strong productivity growth from 1993–94 to 1998–99 to be treated as a distinct period, while the weaker years at the beginning of the decade are discarded. The result is a widespread but false impression that the 1990s was a period of exceptionally strong measured MFP growth. In reality, the average rate of MFP growth for two ABS productivity cycles from 1988–89 to 1998–99 was 1.6 per cent—above average but not exceptional compared to preceding decades.

In summary, MFP growth over a productivity cycle is not a particularly useful measure of economic performance. Even when measured correctly, productivity estimates combine the effects of long-term technological growth with a subset of the factors that determine variations in short-term performance. In practice, accurate measurement is impossible. In the case of Australia's supposed productivity surge, the crucial problem is the failure to take account of changes in work intensity.

Work intensity and productivity

Labour productivity is typically measured in terms of output per hour worked. However, this measure can be problematic. For example, enterprise agreements and individual contracts adopted in place of awards commonly eliminate breaks such as tea breaks, which were treated as working time under the award system. On the other hand, employees have always taken unauthorised and unrecorded breaks of various kinds. A notable example that has emerged in the last 10 to 15 years is the use of office computers to visit internet sites that are not work-related. Of much longer standing is the practice of making private phone calls during paid time at work. Conversely, employers may demand unpaid overtime or contact their employees with work requests outside of paid hours.

Although these practices are regularly the subject of dispute, the normal situation is one of equilibrium, in which some deviation from official hours is part of the wage bargain tacitly accepted by both parties. The hours of work reported to statistical agencies will reflect some, but not all, of the deviations from award-determined or contractually agreed hours. How should these features of the labour market be reflected in productivity measures? At least conceptually, it seems clear that the appropriate measure is actual hours worked rather than paid hours.

Consider the case in which the number of hours worked remains unchanged, but the pace of work varies. In some industries, such changes can be observed directly and are the subject of explicit wage bargaining. The archetypal case is that of production-line work, in which employers typically seek to increase the rate at which the line moves, while workers and unions try to slow it down. The development of the word processor in the 1980s provides another example. Since the number of keystrokes could be measured directly, employers demanded higher rates, thus precipitating an epidemic of repetitive strain injury, a problem that had existed previously but was typically diagnosed as an individual pathology rather than a broader occupational hazard.

There is, in principle, no difference between an increase in the number of hours worked and an increase in the pace of work. In both cases, standard economic logic implies that an equilibrium wage bargain will typically involve a commitment of hours and effort greater than the level that would be chosen by workers in the absence of a monetary incentive.

In particular instances, depending on labour market institutions, the bargained outcome may involve more or fewer hours and more or less effort than would characterise a Pareto-optimal bargain. However, the general assumption is that at the margin, increased hours and increased effort are equally costly to workers when they are normalised by the payment required to elicit them. It follows that, to the extent that increases in output are derived either from unmeasured increases in hours of work or from increased intensity of work, there is no corresponding increase in productivity. If the hours or intensity of work were previously sub-optimal (or above the optimal level), there will be a net welfare gain (or loss), but this will be of second-order magnitude relative to the change in output.

Australian economic policymakers have shown considerable confusion on this point. Some have explicitly asserted that working harder is a genuine source of productivity gains. For example, the Productivity Commission (1996, 24) asserted that productivity gains could be achieved not only through resource reallocation but through people 'working harder and working smarter'. More than a decade later, the chairman of the Productivity

Commission repeated an almost identical formulation (Banks 2011 20): 'whether productivity growth comes from working harder or working "smarter", people in workplaces are central to it'. The appearance of scare quotes around 'smarter' is revealing. Whereas in the 1990s this phrase was used in all seriousness, 'working smarter' is now understood as a piece of management jargon, typically decoded as 'We're giving you more work to do with fewer resources, and it's up to you to figure out how to do it.'

The association of reform with harder and less pleasant work is usually implicit. Standard discussions of micro-economic reform and workplace reform are full of references to 'cutting out fat', the 'chill winds of competition' and so forth. It is not hard for workers to discern where there is fat to be cut, or to observe that CEOs are usually equipped with well-padded windbreakers, even in cases where their mismanagement leads to an early (but generously compensated) departure. By contrast, in debates over the validity of MFP statistics, most mainstream economists—particularly those associated with the Productivity Commission—have denied that changes in work intensity are an important source of changes in measured productivity.

The mid-1990s saw an upsurge in public concern about the pace of work, work–life balance, stress and related issues, which persisted into the early 2000s, leading to John Howard's description of the topic at an electorate dinner in Melbourne in 2002 as a 'barbecue stopper' (Treguer 2023). In the context of a strengthening labour market from about 2000 onwards, community resistance to work intensification, and to employer demands for longer hours of work, became increasingly successful.

While the intensity of work is difficult to measure, there is sufficient evidence to support the general perception of an increase in work intensity in the 1990s. First, as discussed above, increases in work hours and in work intensity are substitutes both as inputs to production and as sources of disutility for workers. It follows that, when the equilibrium wage bargain involves an increase (or decrease) in hours, it will also involve an increase (decrease) in work intensity. The data on working hours are unequivocal and exactly consistent with the idea that fluctuations in MFP growth may be explained largely in terms of work intensity. As the ABS (2010) notes, the proportion of full-time workers working more than 50 hours per week increased from 13 per cent in 1978 to 19 per cent in late 1999 and early 2000, before falling to around 15 per cent in 2010.

There is some direct evidence on work intensity. The Australian Workplace Industrial Relations Survey undertaken in 1995 (Morehead et al. 1997) found that a majority of employees reported increases in stress, work effort and pace of work over the previous year, while less than 10 per cent reported reductions in any of these variables. This is consistent with evidence from the UK and some, although not all, other European countries (Green and McIntosh 2001). Moreover, Green and Macintosh observe that the increases in work intensity are associated with higher productivity (as would be expected) and are positively correlated with exposure to competition and reductions in union density.

Defences of the productivity surge

As I have discussed elsewhere (Quiggin 2006), believers in the productivity surge produced a variety of stories to explain the observed outcomes.

Asymmetric measurement error

During the 1990s, the Productivity Commission was the most prominent proponent of the claim that the strong growth in MFP reported by the ABS reflected the emergence of a 'new economy' as a result of micro-economic reform (Parham 1999). Unsurprisingly, the Productivity Commission rejected claims that the apparent surge in MFP growth was due, in part or in whole, to measurement error or cyclical factors.

By contrast, as low rates of MFP growth emerged in the 2000s, the commission became much more sympathetic to the idea that measurement error might be a problem. The poor productivity growth of the early 2000s was blamed on, among other factors, the Sydney Olympics, capital expenditure associated with the Y2K fiasco (also referred to as the Millennium Bug), the transitional effects of the introduction of the GST, and the drought that began in 2002 (Parham 2005). The drought persisted well into the decade, but the other factors should have been transitory.

As measured MFP performance deteriorated even further, attention has shifted to the mining sector. It seems clear that measurement problems associated with mining are significant. Investments in new or expanded mines count immediately as part of the capital stock but contribute to output only with a delay of some years. Moreover, high mineral prices have led to the exploitation of less productive resources that would otherwise be uneconomic.

Since the quality of the resource is not measured as an input, this produces an illusory decline in productivity. Richardson and Denniss (2011) estimate that the measured growth rate of labour productivity over the first decade of the 2000s was reduced by one percentage point as a result of distortions in the mining sector. This is a significant effect, but it is not sufficient to explain the decline in measured MFP growth rates.

The view that the disappointing performance of measured MFP is primarily due to measurement error has gone out of favour over time as disappointment has persisted. However, it frequently re-emerges in discussions of Australia's strong macro-economic performance during and after the GFC.

The idea that market-oriented micro-economic policies provide significant flexibility in response to macro-economic shocks has been influential in Australia since the beginnings of micro-economic reform in the 1980s. This idea contributed substantially to the policy misjudgements that produced the 1989–91 recession, when it was supposed that the economy was flexible enough to handle a 'short, sharp shock to interest rates' and then to bounce back rapidly from 'the recession we had to have'.

Counter-examples to this idea abound. The most striking is that of New Zealand, which has followed broadly similar micro-economic policies since the 1980s, although with more radical micro-economic reform until the mid-1990s and a sharper reaction against some aspects of those policies subsequently. At the same time, New Zealand has adopted far more restrictionist macro-economic policies. From its initial position of approximate income parity with Australia in the early 1980s, New Zealand fell sharply behind, experiencing an even deeper recession from 1987 to 1991 and two subsequent recessions interspersed with periods of mostly sluggish growth. By 2000, income per person in New Zealand had fallen to around two-thirds of the Australian level, and it has remained there since. While it is unwise to attribute such a huge gap to any single factor (Hazledine and Quiggin 2006), poor macro-economic performance is an important part of the story.

The lost golden age

The dominant interpretation of the MFP statistics today is of a lost golden age. The surge in measured MFP growth is attributed to the micro-economic reform process that began in the 1980s and the slowing down to 'reform fatigue' in the 2000s.

The major problem with this story is timing. It is difficult to see how a series of reforms undertaken over 20 years or more can have produced substantial productivity benefits confined to a single period of five years. It is even harder to see how the benefits of those reforms can have dissipated so rapidly, having been already on the wane when the reform process was still under way.

The beginning of the process of micro-economic reform is usually dated to the float of the Australian dollar in 1983. There is less agreement on the end of the process. As far as I can determine, I was the first to offer an explicit end date suggesting that the era of micro-economic reform in Australia 'began with a big bang—the floating of the dollar in 1983' and 'ended with another big bang—the package of tax reforms centred on the goods and services tax (GST), which came into force in July 2000' (Quiggin 2004).

There have been retrospective attempts to backdate the end of micro-economic reform, sometimes as far as the election of the Howard government in 1996, but these do not stand up to scrutiny. Although it is true that the Howard government took a less consistent approach to reform than its Labor predecessors, it nevertheless introduced several major reforms in its first few years in office. Many of the reforms implemented under Howard were measures that had long been demanded by advocates of radical reform but resisted by the Labor government because of political sensitivities. These included the *Workplace Relations Act 1996*, the partial privatisation of Telstra in 1998 and 1999, waterfront reform in 1998 and, most notably, the GST, legislated in 1999 and implemented in 2000.[5]

Moreover, many reforms introduced by the Hawke–Keating government did not begin to take effect until after the MFP surge. The most notable of these is the National Competition Policy (NCP). Most states did not even

---

5   Following the surprising achievement of a Senate majority in 2004, the last term of the Howard government included the passage of a package of labour market reforms called *Work Choices*. These reforms were mostly repealed by the Rudd Labor government and cannot be regarded as a successful renewal of micro-economic reform.

complete their legislative reviews or set up their general regulatory bodies until the late 1990s, and the NCP process, with associated payments to the states, was not completed until 2005, when it was succeeded by the National Reform Agenda. Even after 2005, the push for micro-economic reform continued through a proliferation of free-trade agreements, which were less focussed on trade than on constraining government intervention in the domestic economy.

The timing issue becomes more acute when we consider that the measured productivity surge did not begin until a decade after the float of the dollar. In fact, the years during which 'even the resident galah in the pet shop' was talking about micro-economic reform were characterised by the lowest productivity growth of the entire period for which data are available. Hence, the story of the lost golden age relies on the long-delayed benefits of the reforms of the early 1980s, combined with an instant (indeed, in some cases, retrospective) benefit from the reforms of the late 1990s. Even if we were to accept the story of the lost golden age, the whole rationale of micro-economic reform is called into question. Far from generating sustained growth, the lost-golden-age myth suggests that the decade or more of micro-economic reform that began with the floating of the dollar in 1983 produced only five years of above-average productivity growth before requiring a renewed burst of reform merely to sustain past gains.

Conclusion

In the economy of the 21st century, increases in productivity arise almost entirely from capital deepening and improvements in education. Economic theory, therefore, predicts that the rate of MFP growth, properly calculated to take account of labour quality, should be close to zero. This prediction is borne out by the data. Nevertheless, the mythical productivity surge of the mid-1990s continues to dominate the thinking of policymakers, leading to incessant demands for more micro-economic reform to generate higher productivity.

The correlation between demand for higher productivity and increases in work intensity is so evident to most Australians that we take it for granted. What is striking in this context is the failure of (most) Australian economists and economic commentators to accept the evidence on this point. Unlike virtually everyone else in Australia, economists have resolutely denied that the higher measured labour productivity growth evident in the mid-1990s was largely due to increased work intensity, and that the reversal of those measured gains in the 2000 was due to the fact that this intensification could not be sustained.

A belief that large increases in annual productivity growth rates can and should be achieved through micro-economic reform is not supported by the data and can lead to bad public policy decisions. Most notably, the belief lends support to the idea that 'Australians must work harder'. On the contrary, evidence from the labour market is that the work intensification of the 1990s was undesired and unsustainable. Genuine improvements in productivity should permit *reductions* in working hours and work effort, rather than demanding more and harder work.

Bibliography

ABC Radio National. 1989. 'The Treasurer, Paul Keating, has dismissed the call for a tax break on savings and the suggestion of a tax on luxuries'. *PM*. Broadcast, 21 June 1989.

Australian Bureau of Statistics. 2010. '6105.0—Australian Labour Market Statistics, Oct 2010'. www.abs.gov.au/ausstats/abs@.nsf/featurearticlesbyCatalogue/67AB5016DD143FA6CA2578680014A9D9?

Banks, Gary. 2011. 'Successful Reform: Past Lessons, Future Challenges'. Report based on paper presented at Annual Forecasting Conference of the Australian Business Economists, 8 December 2010. Canberra: Productivity Commission.

Bell, Stephen, and John Quiggin. 2006. 'Unemployment, Labour Market Insecurity and Policy Options'. In *Social Policy in Australia: Understanding for Action*, edited by A. McLelland and P. Smyth, 147–60.

Campbell, Simon and Harry Withers. 2017. 'Australian productivity trends and the effect of structural change'. *Economic Roundup*, Australian Treasury, 28 August 2017. treasury.gov.au/publication/p2017-t213722c/.

Dolman, Ben, Lan Lu, and Jyoti Rahman. 2006. 'Understanding Productivity Trends'. *Treasury Economic Roundup*, Summer 2006: 35–52.

Felipe, Jesus, and Franklin Fisher. 2003. 'Aggregation in Production Functions: What Applied Economists Should Know'. *Metroeconomica* 54, no. 2–3: 208–62. doi.org/10.1111/1467-999x.00166.

Green, Francis, and Steve McIntosh. 2001. 'The Intensification of Work in Europe'. *Labour Economics* 8, no. 2: 291–308. doi.org/10.1016/s0927-5371(01)00027-6.

Hazledine, Tim, and John Quiggin. 2006. 'No More Free Beer Tomorrow? Economic Policy and Outcomes in Australia and New Zealand Since 1984'. *Australian Journal of Political Science* 41, no. 2: 145–59. doi.org/10.1080/10361140600672402.

Krugman, Paul. 1997. *The Age of Diminished Expectations: U.S. Economic Policy in the 1990s*, 3rd ed. Cambridge: MIT Press.

Morehead, Alison, Mairi Steele, Michael Alexander, Kerry Stephen, and Linton Duffin. 1997. *Changes at Work: The 1995 Australian Workplace Industrial Relations Survey*. Melbourne: Addison Wesley Longman Australia.

Organisation for Economic Co-operation and Development. 2001. *Measuring Productivity: Measurement of Aggregate and Industry-Level Productivity Growth: OECD Manual*. Paris: Organisation for Economic Co-operation and Development.

Parham, Dean. 1999. *The New Economy? A New Look at Australia's Productivity Performance*. Productivity Commission Staff Research Paper, Ausinfo, Canberra, May 1999. www.pc.gov.au/research/supporting/new-economy/neweconomy.pdf.

Parham, Dean. 2005. 'Is Australia's productivity surge over?'. *Agenda* 12, no. 3: 252–66. doi.org/10.22459/ag.12.03.2005.05.

Parkinson, Martin. 2011. 'Sustaining Growth in Living Standards in the Asian Century'. Paper presented at Melbourne Institute Economic and Social Outlook Conference, Melbourne, 31 June 2011.

Productivity Commission. 1996. *Stocktake of Progress in Microeconomic Reform*. Canberra: Australian Government Publishing Service.

Quiggin, John. 2000. 'Microeconomic Policies and Structural Change-Comments'. In *The Australian Economy in the 1990s*, edited byD. Gruen and S. Shrestha. Sydney: Reserve Bank of Australia.

Quiggin, John. 2004. 'Looking Back on Microeconomic Reform: A Sceptical Viewpoint'. *Economic and Labour Relations Review* 15, no. 1: 1–25. doi.org/10.1177/103530460401500101.

Quiggin, John. 2006. 'Stories about productivity'. *Australian Bulletin of Labour* 32: 18–26.

Quiggin, John. 2011. *The Lost Golden Age of Productivity Growth?* Sydney: Reserve Bank of Australia, 367–77.

Richardson, David, and Richard Denniss. 2011. 'Mining Australia's Productivity: The Role of the Mining Industry in Driving Down Australia's Productivity Growth'. *Policy Brief* 31. Canberra: The Australia Institute.

Solow, Robert. 1956. 'A Contribution to the Theory of Economic Growth'. *Quarterly Journal of Economics* 70, no. 1: 65–94. doi.org/10.2307/1884513.

Tréguer, Pascal. 2021. '"Barbecue Stopper": Meaning and Origin'. word histories, 2021. wordhistories.net/2021/12/15/barbecue-stopper/.

8

Financial markets: masters or servants?

First published in 2011 as Quiggin, John. 'Financial Markets: Masters or Servants?'. *Politics and Society* 39: 331–45. doi.org/10.1177/0032329211 415502.

Trade, and markets of one form or another, have always been part of human society. Borrowing and lending are similarly ancient and ubiquitous. On the other hand, markets for trade in financial obligations such as debts, and future sales and purchases, are specific to capitalism. The key financial institutions of capitalism, such as fractional reserve banking, joint stock companies and regular markets for trade in government bonds, date, in their modern form, from the 18th century. However, precursors can be found as early as the 15th century in Italy and the Netherlands.

Throughout the history of capitalism, there have been tensions between financial institutions and the state, and between financial capital on the one hand, and the firms and households engaged in the production and consumption of physical goods and services on the other. In some periods, most notably in the decades after World War II, financial markets were reduced to a subordinate role, channelling household savings into credit for business investment and (relatively constrained) consumer credit, under tight public regulation. In other periods, including the decades since the 1970s, financial markets became, or at least seemed to become, all-powerful Masters of the Universe.

Periods of financial sector dominance have regularly ended in spectacular panics and crashes, often resulting in the liquidation of large numbers of financial institutions and the reimposition of regulatory controls previously dismissed as outmoded and unnecessary. These panics have typically precipitated lengthy periods of recession or depression, with high unemployment, and slow or negative economic growth.

The financial crisis that engulfed the global economy in 2008 has been, so far, an archetypal example of this process. The power, and pretensions, of financial markets in the decades leading up to the crisis exceeded anything that had been seen in the past. The magnitude of the crisis was similarly impressive, with losses of billions or tens of billions of dollars becoming routine daily events and talk of trillions—commonplace. At several points, it appeared likely that the entire global financial system might collapse, and this danger has not passed at the time of writing (August 2010).

The aim of this paper is to consider measures to restore financial markets to their proper role as servants rather than masters of the market economy and the society within which it is embedded.

The paper is organised as follows. The first section provides a background to the crisis, showing how the Bretton Woods system restricted financial activity and the potential for financial panic. The breakdown of Bretton Woods was followed by a massive expansion in the scale, scope and speculative nature of financial activity. I next describe the Global Financial Crisis (GFC) that began in 2008 and show how it was driven by the complex, interlinked and uncontrolled nature of the financial system. The European sovereign debt crisis of 2010 is a continuation of the global crisis but has been used by financial markets to reassert their power. Section 3 deals with the reform of the international financial system. The central argument is that the idea of a 'global financial architecture' is misconceived. The necessary system is one of national (or EU-level) financial regulation, coordinated through international institutions. In Section 4, I argue that the central goal of national financial regulation should be to constrain the size and power of the financial system to levels appropriate to its role as a provider of services, ultimately dependent on the backing of the state. Finally, I offer some concluding comments.

Background

Periodic financial crises and panics have been a feature of capitalism ever since the South Sea Bubble, which brought an end to the first great experiment with joint-stock corporations. By the 19th century, financial crises replaced crop failures as the primary cause of economic distress. Some notable examples include the Long Depression following the Panic of 1873 in the USA and the 1890s depression in Australia. Kindleberger and Bernstein (2000) provide an extensive list of such crises.

None of these crises, however, were comparable in their effects to the Wall Street Crash of 1929 and the subsequent Great Depression. As well as producing a decade of misery and deprivation, the Depression helped bring Hitler to power in Germany and was therefore a major cause of the Second World War.

Meeting in Bretton Woods, New Hampshire in 1944 to plan a postwar economic order, the Allied governments were determined to avoid a repetition of the disasters of the interwar years. Although the most radical proposals for financial reform, those put forward by John Maynard Keynes, were rejected by the US government, the financial system that emerged from Bretton Woods was far more tightly restricted than any in the past.

The Bretton Woods system supported, and was supported by, Keynesian macro-economic policies, operated at the national level with the aim (largely achieved for several decades) of maintaining full employment, price stability and fiscal balance.

Even during this postwar boom, the financial sector sought and found ways to undermine and avoid controls and regulations. The emergence of the 'Eurodollar' market in the 1960s, which facilitated trade in US dollar-denominated financial instruments outside the control of the US Federal Reserve, was a crucial step in this respect.

After Bretton Woods

The inflationary upsurge of the late 1960s rendered untenable key aspects of the Bretton Woods system, most notably the fixed US-dollar price for gold. Although a variety of responses might have been possible, the gradual erosion of financial controls in the 1960s paved the way for a complete breakdown in the 1970s. Fixed exchange rates were replaced by attempts at flexible management, then by freely floating rates. Controls on international financial flows were relaxed and ultimately abandoned. National financial systems were deregulated (Robinson and Quiggin 1985).

By the 1980s, almost nothing was left of the Bretton Woods system. Governments had little option but to obey the dictates of global financial markets, expressed most notably through the judgements of rating agencies such as Standard & Poor's and Moody's. The volume of international financial flows grew to levels that had previously been unimaginable, and then kept on growing even faster. By some measures, when the bubble burst in 2008, the total outstanding volume of financial assets was over a quadrillion US dollars.

By 2007, financial corporations accounted for 40 per cent of US corporate profits. The bulk of income growth in the USA over the period after the 1970s accrued to high-income earners, an increasing proportion of whom derived their income directly or indirectly from the financial sector. In particular, those in the top 1 per cent of the income distribution approximately doubled their share of income (Piketty and Saez 2003). Within that group, the top 0.1 per cent did disproportionately well. Similar, though less extreme, developments took place throughout the developed world (Atkinson and Leigh 2007; Piketty and Saez 2006).

Nevertheless, by the mid-1990s, the beneficence of financial-sector dominance seemed evident to all, particularly in the USA. Booming stock markets encouraged an atmosphere of triumphalism epitomised by such writers as Thomas Friedman (1999) and Edward Luttwak (1999).

But the first signs of failure were becoming apparent. The global financial system was threatened in 1998 by the failure of Long-Term Capital Management L.P., a hedge fund with leveraged borrowings in the trillions. The danger was averted by a bailout, hastily organised by the US Federal Reserve. The bubble-and-bust in dotcom stocks in the late 1990s repeated the pattern on a larger scale.

Bubble, bust and bailout

Although no one predicted the exact course of the GFC that began in 2008, a substantial minority of economists pointed to the unsustainability of the imbalances in the US economy and the global economy that developed from the late 1990s onwards. They predicted that the resolution of those imbalances would require a painful adjustment and, probably, a recession, followed by more restrictive regulation of the financial system (Bell and Quiggin 2006).

By contrast, the dominant market-liberal ideology encouraged the view that booming asset markets were benign. The massive growth in the volume of international financial transactions was seen as reflecting the (presumptively rational) voluntary choices of borrowers and lenders, and as a way of diversifying risk internationally.

Like other aspects of the financial system that developed during the bubble era, this reasoning was reminiscent of the deacon in Oliver Wendell Holmes's poem of 1858 who tried to build a carriage (the 'wonderful one-hoss shay') that could never break down, on the theory that a system always fails at its weakest spot:

> 'n' the way t' fix it, uz I maintain, is only jest
> To make that place uz strong uz the rest.

> (Holmes 1858)

As applied to the global financial system, the 'one-hoss shay' theory provided two systems of protection against failure. First, risks were widely dispersed throughout the global financial system, so that a localised failure in any one economy could not cause significant loss to investors with highly diversified portfolios. Second, central banks extended 'too-big-to-fail' protection to any institution large enough to be critical to the sustainability of the overall system.

The only way a system of this kind could fail was through a total global collapse. As Holmes, in his poem, described the end of the one-hoss shay:

> [It] went to pieces all at once,—
> All at once, and nothing first,—
> Just as bubbles do when they burst.

> (Holmes 1858)

And that, more or less, is what happened.

In scale and scope, the crisis was larger than any financial failure since the Great Depression. The estimated losses from financial failures amounted to US$4 trillion or about 10 per cent of the world's annual income. Losses in output from the global recession have also amounted to trillions, and recovery has barely begun.

Unlike the Great Depression, this crisis was entirely the product of financial markets. All the checks and balances in the system failed comprehensively. The ratings agencies offered AAA ratings to assets that turned out to be worthless, on the basis of models that assumed that asset prices could never fall. The entire ratings agency model, in which issuers pay for ratings, proved to be fundamentally unsound, but these very ratings were embedded in official systems of regulation. Crucial public policy decisions were, in effect, outsourced to for-profit firms that had a strong incentive to get the answers wrong.

The bailouts undertaken by the US and European governments in late 2008 only reinforced the bad incentives in the system. Financial-sector participants kept most of the rich rewards they had reaped during the bubble years when their activities had massively distorted the allocation of investment capital and thereby reduced the sustainable growth rate of the economy. The terms on which public credit was extended for worthless assets were so generous that the financial sector has led the way in the recovery of corporate profits. Unsurprisingly, given these incentives, the behaviour of the financial sector has changed hardly at all as a result of the crisis.

The European debt crisis

The role of financial markets in the European 'sovereign debt crisis' provides a good illustration of the extent to which the financial sector has reasserted its claims to mastery over the economy. In nearly all respects, the crisis is the result of the financial excesses of the bubble era and the costly misallocation of resources it created.

Many of the European governments most severely affected by the crisis were in fiscal balance or surplus in 2007. The slide into deficit can be attributed to:

- the direct and indirect costs of financial sector bailouts (most notable in Ireland)
- the loss of revenue from the financial sector and from housing following the bursting of the bubble (most notable in Spain)
- the fiscal impact of the general economic downturn and the cost of stimulus and relief measures.

Even in Greece, where fiscal profligacy was a primary cause of the crisis, financial enterprises were both leading accomplices in the evasion of Eurozone fiscal targets and leading beneficiaries of the EU bailout. While ordinary Greeks have been forced to accept austerity measures, the US, German and French banks that made unsound loans can expect to be paid in full.

Yet the financial sector has presented itself as the guardian of fiscal probity, with rating agencies downgrading public debt and bond markets demanding cuts in public expenditure, invariably targeted at those who benefited least from the bubble.[1] The most striking examples include the UK, where the cost of the bank bailout is being used to justify ever-harsher treatment of the homeless and unemployed, and Ireland, where the government plans to sell most of the assets of the National Pension Reserve Fund (created to finance public service and social welfare pensions) to pay off creditors of failed private banks. Elsewhere in Europe, 'austerity' proposals have generally been more reasonable, with a primary focus on proposals to enhance tax revenue and measures to reduce the cost of retirement income policies, in most cases by increasing the age of retirement.

Budgets must balance in the long run, and policies of this kind are, to some extent, a necessary response to a real reduction in the net worth of governments as a result of the financial crisis. Nevertheless, the demands of the financial sector for austerity have produced an undesirable focus on measures to reduce budget deficits in the short term, at a time when the depressed state of the European economy implies the need for stimulus.

A striking example is that of the increases in Value Added Tax (VAT) rates adopted in Spain, Portugal and other European countries. A far more sensible policy would have been to announce an increase in the VAT rate, deferred for two to three years. The effect on long-term fiscal balance would be only marginally smaller than that of an immediate increase. On the other hand, a deferred increase would stimulate demand in the short-term, as consumers seek to beat the tax increase. Such a temporary stimulus is exactly what is needed.

---

1   A particularly striking example of the financial sector's unwillingness to learn from experience was that of Timothy Ash of the Royal Bank of Scotland. Speaking about the IMF rescue package for Ukraine, Ash observed 'We hope the fund is maintaining its push for a more flexible exchange rate, far-reaching reforms in the banking sector, and more privatization' (quoted in Krasnolutska and Martens 2008). A few weeks before this comment was made, RBS had been nationalised as a result of failed speculation and catastrophic mismanagement.

Reforming the international financial system

The aftermath of the crisis has produced a range of efforts to improve upon the systems of financial regulation that failed so spectacularly in 2007 and 2008. The most important instance is that of the proposed Basel III Accords on banking supervision. The draft rules reverse many of the presumptions that informed the 'light-handed' approach of the Basel II system, which failed spectacularly in the global crisis. Basel III involves a substantial increase in bank capital requirements. More importantly, the risk-based framework of Basel II, in which banks were largely free to make their own judgements about the riskiness of their capital base, has been replaced by more prescriptive requirements to hold specific capital assets.

These efforts have not, however, been informed by any rethinking of the role of the financial sector. As a result, they amount to an attempt to repair and recreate the pre-crisis system, fixing the obvious defects while maintaining the status of the financial sector as the core of economic activity. Ideally, in this view, the financial sector would retain its role of mastery over investment decisions and public policy while avoiding the excesses of the past.

Such an approach is doomed to failure. Even while the crisis was at its worst, there were regular examples of excess, such as massive payouts and lavish junkets for executives of bailed-out banks. Now that, for the financial sector at least, the crisis is effectively over, the return to pre-crisis attitudes and behaviour is gathering pace.

Starting from the view of the financial sector as a servant of the broader economy and society rather than as a master would produce a radically different approach to its regulation. A whole series of presumptions that have characterised the failed regulatory approaches of recent decades would be reversed. Most notably:

- The financial sector should be regarded as the biggest single source of economic risk rather than the pre-eminent social institution for risk management.
- Financial innovation should be regarded as harmful unless it can be shown to be beneficial, rather than vice versa.
- Growth in the financial sector share of the economy should be regarded with concern rather than celebration.

- Financial markets must be regulated as interlinked national markets rather than as a global market transcending national boundaries.

A successful approach to global financial regulation must rely primarily on co-operation between the US Federal Reserve and the European Central Bank (ECB), which between them account for more than 90 per cent of currency reserves and economies producing around a third of global output. Although the UK and Japan remain significant financial centres, the severe fiscal and regulatory problems they face suggest that they are unlikely to be in a position to play an independent role in the restructuring of the global financial system for some time to come. Other members of the G20 are similarly constrained.

Financial innovation

The process of financial innovation, involving either the creation of new financial instruments or the design of new financial strategies for firms (often termed 'financial engineering') was a central feature of the era of neoliberalism. The growth of finance has been almost unstoppable. Seemingly major financial crises like the stock market crash of 1987 or the Nasdaq[2] crash of 2000 stimulated the development of yet more innovative responses. Even the exposure of spectacular fraud at the Enron Corporation, which had been named by Fortune magazine as 'America's most innovative' for six years in succession, did little to dent faith in the desirability of innovation.

It is now clear that unrestricted financial innovation played a major role in the advent of the financial crisis by facilitating the growth of unsound lending and undermining systems of regulation. There is an inherent inconsistency between unrestricted financial innovation and a regulatory system aimed at preventing the failure of financial systems or insuring market participants against such failures. Guarantees create 'moral hazard' by allowing financial institutions to capture the benefits of risky investments while shifting some or all the losses to government-backed insurance pools.

Moral hazard can only be offset by the design of regulatory mechanisms that discourage excessive risk-taking. However, as the literature on mechanism design has shown, the effectiveness of such mechanisms depends on the existence of stable relationships between the observable

---

2   National Association of Securities Dealers Automated Quotations Stock Market.

variables that are the subject of regulation and the risk allocation that generates these observables. Financial innovation changes the relationship. In the presence of moral hazard, therefore, there is an incentive to introduce innovations that increase the underlying level of risk while leaving regulatory measures of risk unchanged.

It follows that the only sustainable approach to financial innovation is one in which proposed innovations are introduced only after the implementation of necessary changes to regulatory requirements and risk measures. If reliable risk measures cannot be computed, the associated innovations should not be permitted.

Obviously, this approach is directly opposed to the Basel II system, which sought to control the total risk exposure of regulated banks while maximising the freedom of financial institutions to benefit from financial innovation. The failure of that system is reflected in the substantially more prescriptive approach of Basel III. However, despite the substantial tightening of restrictions in Basel III, the underlying presumption in favour of financial innovation remains. It is this presumption that needs to be reversed if financial regulation is to be effective.

Controlling risk in the financial sector

Given an unlimited public guarantee for the liabilities of these institutions, a permissive attitude to innovation is a guaranteed, and proven, recipe for disaster, offering huge rewards to any innovation that increases both risks (ultimately borne by the public) and returns (captured by the innovators).

Post-crisis financial regulation must begin with a clearly defined set of institutions (such as banks and insurance companies) offering a set of well-tested financial instruments with explicit public guarantees for clients and a public guarantee of solvency, with nationalisation as a last-resort option. Financial innovations must be treated with caution and allowed only when there is a clear understanding of their effects on systemic risk.

In this context, it is crucial to maintain sharp boundaries between publicly guaranteed institutions and unprotected financial institutions such as hedge funds, finance companies, stockbroking firms and mutual funds. Institutions in the latter category must not be allowed to present a threat of systemic failure that might precipitate a public sector rescue, whether direct (as in the recent crisis) or indirect (as in the 1998 bailout of Long-Term Capital Management). A number of measures are required to ensure this.

First, ownership links between protected and unprotected financial institutions must be absolutely prohibited, to avoid the risk that the failure of an unregulated subsidiary will necessitate a rescue of the parent, or that an unregulated parent could seek to expose a bank subsidiary to excessive risk. Long before the current crisis, these dangers were illustrated by Australian experience with bank-owned finance companies, most notably the rescue, by the Reserve Bank of Australia, of the Bank of Adelaide in the 1970s.

Second, banks should not deal in unregulated financial products such as share investments and hedge funds.

Third, the provision of bank credit to unregulated financial enterprises should be limited to levels that ensure that even large-scale failure in this sector cannot threaten the solvency of the regulated system.

In the resulting system of 'narrow banking', the financial sector would become, in effect, an infrastructure service, like electricity or telecommunications. While the provision of financial services might be undertaken by either public or private enterprises, governments would accept a clear responsibility for the stability of the financial infrastructure.

Another important regulatory adjustment will be the end of the system by which prudential regulation has been, in effect, outsourced to ratings agencies such as Standard & Poor's and Moody's. Agency ratings have been enshrined in regulation: for example, official investment guidelines require regulated entities to invest in assets with a high rating (AAA in some cases, investment grade in others) or provide those responsible for making bad investment decisions with a safe harbour against claims of negligence if the assets in question carried a high rating. For these purposes at least, an international, publicly backed non-profit system of assessing and rating investments is required.

Constraining the size of the financial sector

The first objective must be to ensure that exchange rate movements reflect the economic fundamentals of trade and long-term capital flows rather than the vicissitudes of financial markets. The most promising strategy for achieving this goal is the idea, long-advocated and long-resisted, of a small tax on financial transactions, commonly called a Tobin tax, after its proposer (Tobin 1988; see also ul Haq, Grunberg, and Kaul 1996).

A tax at a rate of 0.1 per cent would be insignificant in relation to the transaction costs associated with international trade or long-term investments. On the other hand, daily transactions of US$3 trillion would yield revenue of US$30 billion per day, or nearly US$1 trillion per year. Since this amount exceeds the total profits of the financial sector, an effective Tobin tax would imply a drastic reduction in the volume of short-term financial flows. It follows that the revenue from a Tobin tax, while significant, would not be sufficient to replace the main existing sources of taxation, such as income tax.

The large volume of literature on the Tobin tax has identified some problems with the simple proposal for a tax on international financial transactions. First, it is possible to replicate spot transactions on foreign exchange markets with combinations of forward transactions and futures, and swap transactions. To make a Tobin tax effective, it would have to be applied to all financial transactions, including domestic transactions. During the bubble era, when the few remaining taxes on domestic financial transactions were being scrapped to facilitate the growth of the financial sector, this was seen as a fatal objection. It has become apparent, however, that the destabilising effects of explosive growth in the volume of financial transactions are much the same whether the transactions are domestic or international.

The fact that a Tobin tax on international financial transactions would be integrated with taxes on domestic transactions suggests that, in all probability, revenue would be collected and retained by national governments. However, suggestions that at least some of the revenue could be used to fund global projects such as the international development goals of the United Nations Conference on Trade and Development (UNCTAD) remain worthy of consideration.

The second problem is that the tax would require global cooperation to prevent financial market activity from migrating to jurisdictions that did not apply the tax. Although this will remain a problem in the post-crisis world, it is likely to be much less severe than indicated by earlier discussions. The number of separate jurisdictions that would need to agree has been substantially diminished by the emergence of the euro.

As part of the resolution of the crisis, it seems inevitable that most remaining European currencies, with the possible exception of the British pound, will disappear, and that a Europe-wide regulatory system will emerge. The number of separate jurisdictions with well-developed financial systems is, therefore, likely to be very small, with the European Union (EU) and the USA being overwhelmingly dominant. Furthermore, successful resolution of the sovereign debt crisis will involve a substantial and growing role for fiscal transfers within the Eurozone. Thus, the EU will become more and more comparable to the USA in economic terms.

As in the case of tax evasion, the problem of 'offshore' financial centres such as Caribbean island states is unlikely to be a serious stumbling block. The free-market dogmas that prevented action to preserve the effectiveness of financial regulation in the late 20th century have lost much of their force. A Tobin tax on transactions among complying jurisdictions may have to be supplemented by a punitive tax at a rate of, say, 10 per cent on transactions with non-compliant jurisdictions. This would ensure that non-compliant jurisdictions were excluded from global financial markets, though the penalty would be modest as regards trade and long-term investment flows.

The new financial architecture: global or international?

The first step towards a sustainable financial architecture is the recognition that the idea of a global financial architecture is both misleading and unattainable. The starting point for any financial architecture must be the institution that acts as lender of last resort for others. This function is, and is likely to remain, one undertaken by national governments and their central banks.[3] It follows that there can be no global financial architecture. Rather, national systems of financial regulation must be linked and integrated to produce a sustainable international financial architecture.

The first requirement for such an architecture is that there should be no 'offshore' financial system that is outside the agreements governing the international financial architecture but nevertheless allowed to transact with institutions inside the system.

---

3   The Eurozone, where national governments run their own prudential policies but share a common central bank, raises some interesting questions but is unlikely to serve as a model for the rest of the world.

This issue has already arisen in relation to international tax avoidance and evasion, and it will arise in an even more acute form in relation to the Tobin tax, discussed below. Fortunately, the Organisation for Economic Co-operation and Development (OECD) has already made substantial progress on tax avoidance, and the approach here will serve as a model for financial regulation.

The OECD prepared an internationally agreed tax standard allowing countries to choose their own tax rates but requiring the exchange of information to prevent avoidance and evasion. Jurisdictions that implemented the standard were placed on a white list, while those that refused were placed on a black list. Countries that promised to implement the standard but had not yet done so were placed on a grey list. Blacklisted jurisdictions were threatened with sanctions, largely unspecified but sufficiently effective that, by October 2009, no jurisdictions surveyed by the OECD global forum remained on the blacklist.

The tax standard is inadequate in many respects, and open to the evasive tactics for which tax havens are famous. Nevertheless, it seems clear that standards will be tightened progressively, and that no jurisdiction will be willing to risk the consequences of refusal to implement them.

The Financial Stability Board, established after the 2009 G20 London summit to strengthen prudential oversight of capital, liquidity and risk management, provides the potential to apply the tax haven model to 'regulatory havens' offering lax financial regulation. As with taxation, the process will undoubtedly be slow. Nevertheless, the powers of the G20 financial regulators are sufficient to ensure that evasion of financial regulation through the use of offshore transactions can be prevented. It remains to be seen whether, in the absence of immediate crisis, governments will find the political will required to resist the demands of financial institutions for light-handed regulation.

These new developments raise fundamental questions about the role of existing international organisations, most importantly the International Monetary Fund (IMF). The IMF has historically acted to preserve the interests and power of the global financial sector. IMF interventions, presented as 'bailouts' of indebted countries, have typically imposed terms only marginally more favourable to the country concerned than the outcomes they would incur through default. The real beneficiaries have been lenders. After a brief conversion to policies of Keynesian stimulus in the deepest phase of the GFC, the IMF is again acting as an advocate of 'austerity' in the interests of bondholders.

The World Bank and the regional development banks also have an important role to play in countercyclical responses to financial crises. The experience of the recent crisis showed the need for more rapid and flexible responses.

The outcomes of the 1990s bubble economy

Like previous episodes of finance-dominated capitalism, the bubble economy that emerged in the 1990s has ended in disaster and depression. Despite the support of sophisticated economic theories, best practice national and international regulation, and the almost unbounded information flows made possible by technological advances in computing and telecommunications, the global financial sector has proved to be just as vulnerable to fraud and failure today as in the days of the South Sea Bubble. Economically and socially sustainable growth will be possible only if the financial sector is forced back into the role of servant rather than master. This will not be easy to achieve. Despite their spectacular collective failure and evident dependence on government handouts for survival, the leaders of the financial sector remain both wealthy and powerful. So far, they have successfully resisted all but the most limited encroachments on their power and freedom.

They have, however, lost their most important asset: the aura of infallibility that surrounded 'the markets'. While ordinary citizens may find it difficult to conceive an alternative to financial market dominance, they no longer believe that a finance-dominated economy ultimately works for the benefit of all. Given a properly articulated program of reform, it should be possible to mobilise sufficient public support and anger to overwhelm the defences raised by these 21st-century 'malefactors of great wealth'.[4]

---

4   The phrase was coined by US President Theodore Roosevelt in an address on the occasion of the laying of the cornerstone of the Pilgrim Monument, Provincetown, Massachusetts, 20 August 1907. Theodore Roosevelt Digital Library. Dickinson State University. www.theodorerooseveltcenter.org/Research/Digital-Library/Record.aspx?libID=o286435.

Bibliography

Atkinson, Anthony, and Andrew Leigh. 2007. 'The Distribution of Top Incomes in Australia. *Economic Record* 83, no. 262: 247–61. doi.org/10.1111/j.1475-4932. 2007.00412.x.

Bell, Stephen, and John Quiggin. 2006. 'Asset Price Instability and Policy Responses: The Legacy of Liberalization'. *Journal of Economic Issues* 40, no. 3: 629–49. doi.org/10.1080/00213624.2006.11506938.

Friedman, Thomas. 1999. *The Lexus and the Olive Tree: Understanding Globalization*. New York: Farrar, Strauss and Giroux.

Holmes, Oliver Wendell. 1858. 'The Wonderful One-Hoss Shay'. *The Atlantic Monthly* (September 1858). Reproduced in Oliver Wendell Holmes, Sr. 1897. *The Wonderful One-Hoss Shay and Other Poems*. New York: Frederick A. Stokes Company. Project Gutenberg E-Book. Last modified 18 February 2018. www.gutenberg.org/files/45280/45280-h/45280-h.htm.

Kindleberger, Charles, and Peter Bernstein. 2000. *Manias, Panics and Crashes: A History of Financial Crises*. New York: John Wiley and Sons. doi.org/10.1057/9780230536753.

Luttwak, Edward. 1999. *Turbo Capitalism: Winners and Losers in the Global Economy*. New York: Harper Collins. doi.org/10.2307/20049379.

Piketty, Thomas and Emanuel Saez. 2003. 'Income Inequality in the United States, 1913–1998*'. *Quarterly Journal of Economics* 118, no. 1: 1–39. doi.org/10.1162/00335530360535135.

Piketty, Thomas, and Emanuel Saez. 2006. 'The Evolution of Top Incomes: A Historical and International Perspective'. *American Economic Review* 96, no. 2: 200–05. doi.org/10.1257/000282806777212116.

Robinson, Marc, and John Quiggin. 1985. 'Retreat from Social Control: Financial Deregulation Since World War II'. *Journal of Australian Political Economy* 18: 9–16.

Quiggin, John. 2011. 'Financial Markets: Masters or Servants?'. *Politics and Society* 39: 331–45. doi.org/10.1177/0032329211415502.

Tobin, James. 1988. 'International Monetary Reform: Sand in the Wheels'. For *Neue Zürcher Zeitung*, July 1988.

ul Haq, Mahbub, Isabelle Grunberg, and Inge Kaul. 1996. *The Tobin Tax: Coping with Financial Volatility*. Oxford: Oxford University Press.

9

Basic or universal? Pathways for a universal basic income

The idea of a universal basic income (UBI) has been around for a long time. However, it has seized the imagination of large sections of the public only very recently, in the wake of the Global Financial Crisis (GFC) and the subsequent political upheavals.

Basic income concepts have been advanced in a range of forms, and in support of radically different political agendas. As a result, it has acquired a highly disparate group of supporters and a disparate group of opponents. For example, the idea of a negative income tax is most commonly favoured by advocates of free markets, while the left has been more attracted to a universal payment or 'demogrant'. More incremental reform programs have been associated with the concept of a guaranteed minimum income.

A crucial but not well understood starting point for analysis is that, when fully implemented, all these proposals are equivalent in terms of their effects on the ultimate distribution of income. Any universal grant financed by taxation can be replicated by a negative income tax, or by a means-test guaranteed minimum income.

The sharp differences between advocates of different versions of universal basic income reflect the broader political visions with which they are associated and the rhetorical framing of the proposals. For a variety of reasons, many of the most ardent supporters of a universal basic income are more excited by the first term, 'universal', than by the second, 'basic'. 'Basic' reflects the idea that everyone should receive a payment, even if it is initially too small to support an adequate standard of living. However, as will be argued in this chapter, any feasible route to a UBI must begin by focussing on 'basic'; that is, on ensuring that all those whose market income is inadequate receive enough to provide a basic standard of living.

Varieties of universal basic income

This section begins by defining the three versions of universal basic income: a guaranteed minimum income, a negative income tax and a universal grant. Section 2.1 begins with the observation that, except for the age requirement, Australia's retirement income system meets the requirements for a UBI. The age pension is set at a level sufficient to lift all people of eligible age out of poverty. Concessions on superannuation mean that virtually everyone receives public support equal to, or greater than, the value of the pension. In these respects, the age pension contrasts markedly with other existing benefits. Section 1.3 provides the starting point for any comparative analysis, namely, a demonstration that any universal grant financed by taxation can be replicated by a negative income tax, or by a means-tested guaranteed minimum income.

Definitions

The core feature of any UBI proposal is an unconditional commitment to ensuring that all members of the community have an income sufficient to sustain a basic standard of living that the community has agreed is acceptable.

A universal basic income is an unconditional amount paid to everyone in the community. The UBI could be paid to individuals or families, and could be varied to take into account special needs such as disability.

A guaranteed minimum income (GMI) is a policy that ensures that everyone in the community receives an income sufficient to sustain a basic standard of living. Although a UBI meets this criterion, a GMI is typically assumed to be paid only to those whose market income is inadequate.

A negative income tax (NIT) is a specific way of implementing the GMI, with a tax schedule that includes a positive payment, equal to the guaranteed minimum for those with zero income. As income rises, the payment is reduced pro rata until income reaches the point where positive amounts of tax must be paid. Commonly, the tax rate is assumed to be flat. The NIT is most closely associated with free-market economists such as Milton Friedman, its primary appeal being that it would replace social welfare payments.

Finally, a universal grant, sometimes called a 'demogrant', is an unconditional payment to all members of the community. Advocates of universal grants commonly use the term 'universal basic income' to describe this policy and claim that alternative versions such as GMI and NIT cannot properly be described as UBI policies. While rhetorically effective in some contexts, such a claim is not helpful as a starting point for analysis, since it constitutes an argument by definition rather than a demonstration that a particular version of the policy is superior. Moreover, the fact that all of these policies are (or may be made) effectively equivalent in terms of their effects on the distribution of income, as shown in Section 3.1, casts doubt on claims that seem to imply a fundamental difference between them.

A universal grant may be of any size and need not be large enough to sustain a standard of living. The Alaska Permanent Fund Dividend, supported by oil revenues, is an example. The fund, which began operations in 1982, paid out about US$2,500 to every Alaskan resident in 2015.

Retirement income

As an example of a commitment to provide a basic income, consider retirement income. In Australia, as in most developed countries, everyone who has reached a certain age receives an income sufficient to keep them out of poverty, at least according to generally accepted measures such as the Henderson poverty line. The basic commitment is implemented through the age pension, which is set, for an individual, at 27.7 per cent of Male Total Average Weekly Earnings (MTAWE)[1]. Further adjustments are made for differences in circumstances. Most importantly, recipients who rent privately receive assistance that depends on their household structure and rental payments.

The age pension is subject to a means test on income and assets. However, the thresholds are high enough, and the clawback rates low enough, that anyone for whom they are relevant can attain a standard of living comparable to that of typical working-age households. Moreover, taking

---

1   Following a long series of gradual increases, the pension age is now 67. A proposal for a further increase to age 70 was abandoned by the Abbott government but may be revived in the future.

superannuation concessions into account, the total value of the benefit provided to 'self-funded' retirees exceeds, in most cases, the value of the age pension. The means test simply limits double dipping.

The social commitment to provision of a basic income does not extend to people of working age, or to children. Social security benefits for these groups are conditional on stringent tests for disability, active job search and other factors, as well as income and asset tests that can only be resolved positively by people below or near the poverty line. Moreover, most benefits are fixed at levels too low to keep recipients out of poverty. In particular, the unemployment benefit, now called NewStart allowance (the similarity to Orwell's Newspeak is presumably unintentional) has been frozen in real terms since 1994 and is well below the poverty line.

Equivalence

A crucial fact about the policies described above is that, in terms of their effects on the final distribution of income, they are all equivalent. That is, any universal grant financed by taxation can be replicated by a negative income tax, or by a means-tested guaranteed minimum income.

This point may be illustrated by a simplified example in which we disregard households and assume that everyone in the community is treated as a separate individual for the purpose of tax and welfare payments. Consider a community in which average annual market income per person is A$100,000 and the acceptable basic income is set at A$25,000.

A universal payment of A$25,000 could, therefore, be financed by a proportional income tax set at a rate of 25 per cent. Someone with no market income would receive the payment and pay no tax, so that net income would be equal to A$25,000. Someone earning an average income of A$100,000 would receive A$25,000 in universal payment and pay A$25,000 in tax, ending up with an unchanged net income of A$100,000. Someone earning A$200,000 would pay A$50,000 in tax and have a net income of A$175,000.

It is easy to see that the same outcome could be achieved with a negative income tax, also at a rate of 25 per cent, with the payment at zero income set at A$25,000. This tax would raise zero net revenue but would yield the same post-tax incomes as the universal payment described above.

Finally, consider a means-tested guaranteed minimum income set at A$25,000, with a clawback rate of 25 per cent. Everyone with incomes under A$100,000 would receive a payment. The payment could be financed by a single-bracket income tax with a threshold of A$100,000 and a marginal tax rate of 25 per cent.

These three policies would have identical effects on the distribution of income after taxes and transfers. Each would also imply that everyone in the community faced an effective marginal tax rate (some of the marginal tax rate and the clawback rate for means-tested benefits) of 25 per cent. On the other hand, they would have radically different effects on the ratio of government revenue to national income. The universal payment would imply setting government revenue and expenditure equal to 25 per cent of income, while, as noted, the negative income tax would raise no net revenue and require no expenditure.

The revenue and expenditure associated with a means-tested, guaranteed minimum income would depend on how unequally incomes were distributed around the mean value of A$100,000.

Based on plausible simplifying assumptions, the required expenditure and revenue would be between 7.5 and 12.5 per cent of national income. Polar cases include:

1. A uniform distribution over the range [0, 100,000]. This distribution implies a revenue and expenditure requirement equal to 12.5 per cent of national income.

2. A three-point distribution, with 30 per cent receiving zero, 40 per cent receiving A$100,000 and 30 per cent receiving A$200,000. This distribution implies a revenue and expenditure requirement equal to 7.5 per cent of national income.

As these examples illustrate, the difference between means-testing and taxation is essentially arbitrary. This means that, in the present context, measures of the ratio of tax revenue and public expenditure to national income do not tell us much. Depending on the administrative systems involved, the various proposals described above might have different implications for compliance and other factors. However, in a fully integrated tax–welfare system, these distinctions would disappear.

Admittedly, this equivalence is only valid when the schemes are implemented in full. If we are considering at transition from the current situation to a universal basic income, there are genuine distinctions between the alternative approaches.

Universal first or basic first?

As a vision of the future, there's plenty of appeal in the idea of a society in which everyone has sufficient resources to meet their basic needs, regardless of their assets, abilities or the way they choose to live their lives. Yet, once we return to the realm of electoral politics, the unavoidable question arises: how do we get there from here? Given the obvious impossibility of implementing a UBI in one or a few terms of governments, what should be the first steps?

Universal first

Intuitively, a priority on universalism leads to the idea that we should begin with a small demogrant, which would gradually increase in value to the point where it becomes sufficient to meet basic needs. Alaska's Permanent Fund Dividend, paid out of the invested proceeds of oil royalties, is often cited as an exemplar of this approach. The fund paid each Alaskan around US$2,100 in 2015 (Widerquist 2015), one of the highest amounts ever, reflecting high oil prices in the previous year.

Unfortunately, US$2,500 a year is only about US$40 a week, a handy addition to the budget but not nearly enough for a person to live on. In the absence of independent income (say, from private investments), the number of Alaskans who have been freed from the need to work, or meet the demanding conditions for unemployment benefits, is approximately zero.

Nor is there any real prospect that this will change. Even if the dividend were to double or triple, it would not provide a poverty line income as defined by the US government, let alone a decent living standard. And, in the absence of an unlikely oil bonanza, there's no reason to expect any increase at all.

In practical terms, a strategy of starting with a small universal benefit, and gradually increasing it, can yield no real impact for several decades. Over the course of such a period, it is likely that some real or imagined budgetary emergency would see the program curtailed and ultimately scrapped. This has already happened in the case of Alaska's Permanent Fund.

In 2017, the Alaskan legislature voted to allocate some of the funds to offsetting the state's budget deficit rather than using it to finance the Dividend. The result was a reduction in the annual dividend of US$1,250 (Brooks 2017).

To avoid these risks, a universal-first approach requires the immediate introduction of a universal payment substantial enough to support at least a minimal standard of living. This, in turn, would require a substantial increase in tax rates, introduced at a stroke. While the impact on net income would be offset by the existence of the universal grant, the difficulties in specifying a new tax scale, and adjusting tax concessions, in such a way as to spread the burden equitably would be formidable. Political aspects of the problem are discussed below.

Basic first

The alternative is to start with 'basic' rather than 'universal'. That is, begin by providing sufficient income to support a decent standard of living to those most in need, then expand it to the entire population. This approach is most naturally associated with a guaranteed minimum income.

Existing benefit systems potentially fall short of the GMI in three ways. First, each benefit in the system is conditional on eligibility requirements such as disability or job search activity. Second, they are subject to clawbacks that imply high effective marginal rates of taxation. Finally, with exceptions such as the old age pension, these benefits are typically insufficient to lift recipients out of poverty.

Since the 1990s, access to basic incomes has become steadily more difficult in all these respects. The case of unemployment benefits, noted above, is typical. Similar cuts and restrictions have been imposed on disability benefits, and supporting parents benefits, in Australia and elsewhere in the world. These cuts have been driven by a combination of neoliberal drives to reduce public spending[2] and conservative hostility to welfare recipients, reflected in the use of stigmatising terms such as 'dole bludgers'.[3]

---

2 The seemingly uncontroversial statement that a substantial and permanent increase in public expenditure must be financed by a similar increase in taxation frequently leads to objections put forward on the basis of Modern Monetary Theory, an updating of the 'functional finance' ideas of Lerner (1943). Quiggin (2011) is a response.

3 Such rhetoric typically involves a mixture of downwards class envy and age-based prejudices. Programs such as 'work for the dole' are invariably introduced for young workers first, before being extended to unemployed workers in general.

A 'basic first' approach would require reversing these trends and would, therefore, entail immediate and sharp political division between advocates of a basic income and supporters of the push to restrict welfare benefits to the 'deserving poor'. Political implications are discussed in more detail in Section 4.

How to get there

Assuming a 'basic first' approach is preferred. How might it be implemented? As initial steps, three measures might be considered:

1. increasing unemployment benefits, at least to the poverty line
2. replacing the job search test for unemployment benefits with a 'participation test'
3. fully integrating the tax and welfare systems.

Increasing unemployment benefits

The basic age pension in Australia is around 28 per cent of MTAWE for single pensioners and 42 per cent for couples. This income has proved sufficient to eliminate, almost completely, poverty among the old, who were once the most exposed to privation. The same level applies to service pensions and disability support pensions.

By contrast, unemployment benefits (now given the Newspeaky name Newstart) were briefly set equal to old pensions at 25 per cent of MTAWE under the Whitlam government. However, a long series of cuts and freezes have reduced access to benefits and cut their relative value to around 18 per cent of MTAWE today.

Participation income

While social acceptance for a completely unconditional basic income is a long way off, a 'participation income' as proposed by Atkinson would have many of the same effects. The criteria for earning a basic income would no longer be based on market production but on a social assessment of value. Participation in this context would include full-time study, raising children and voluntary work. Over time, it might be extended to encompass commitments to artistic, cultural and sporting endeavours, even if these were not at a level sufficient to generate a market income or qualify for existing forms of public support.

A fully integrated tax–welfare system

As discussed above, a fully implemented universal basic income would imply an integrated tax–welfare system, in which the distinction between means testing and taxation would disappear. A step towards this goal would be the inclusion of benefit payments in taxable income, with a corresponding, or larger, reduction in clawback rates.

Completely integrating clawbacks into the tax system would clarify the effective marginal tax rates currently faced by benefit recipients (commonly above 60 per cent). This would provide a counterargument to the spurious claims that the marginal rate faced by high-income earners (less than 50 per cent) constitutes an unreasonable disincentive to work.

Utopianism, managerialism and reform

We have moved from a situation in which the left offered a utopian vision that inspired people to one in which centre-left parties have offered a manageralist response to the GFC and the rise of inequality. That has proved insufficient to mobilise and engage people or to stave off the 'dominant identity politics'[4] that has largely supplanted neoliberalism on the right. We need to recapture the vision and language of utopia that used to be part and parcel of left politics.

The light on the hill

As the discussion above suggests, UBI is not a short-term policy option but a vision to be realised over the coming decades. Therefore, the crucial issues concern not the details of the design but the process and politics of getting there.

---

4   Commonly referred to as 'populism', dominant identity politics has emerged as a central theme of right-wing politics in many countries. The starting point is an assumed 'representative identity' for 'everyday citizens' of the country concerned. The representative 'everyday Australian (or American)' is taken to be white, English-speaking, Christian, heterosexual, employed or retired, and, at least by default, male.

This distinction between a short-term policy platform and a long-term objective used to be normal for social democratic and socialist parties, and it was long reflected in the unwillingness of members of the Australian Labor Party (ALP) to discard the socialist objective,[5] even after decades in which Labor governments were more likely to privatise than nationalise.

For the future, we need more than a formal set of words in a policy platform. We need, in Chifley's words, a 'light on the hill' towards which we can climb year by year. In this context, it is useful to compare, once again, the 'basic-first' and 'universal-first' approaches.

A basic-first approach to universal basic income requires the reversal of longstanding trends that have tightened access to unemployment benefits and other forms of welfare. It therefore involves a direct assault on the policy directions that have prevailed for at least the past 25 years. It links an ultimate, currently unattainable objective to immediate political struggles.

A universal-first approach is more explicitly utopian in its vision than the basic-first approach. However, there is no obvious starting point for a short-term fighting platform.

Beyond the labour market

For most people, the central fact of economic life is the need to work for a living by producing, or helping to produce, goods and services that can be sold in a market. That is true not only of work for wages but of the domestic work, mostly done by women, that must be done to make market work possible. It is also true of most of those who are formally classified as self-employed, and many small employers.

To put it simply, having a job is a vital economic necessity. To maintain a moderately comfortable life, we need not just a job but a full-time job, with good wages and reasonable security. Moreover, except for a relatively brief period in the mid-20th century (the Keynesian 'long boom'), the existence of enough jobs to provide employment for the workforce has depended on the willingness and ability of owners of capital to provide those jobs.

---

5   The ALP National Constitution states that '[t]he Australian Labor Party is a democratic socialist party and has the objective of the democratic socialisation of industry, production, distribution and exchange, to the extent necessary to eliminate exploitation and other anti-social features in these fields.' This wording has remained unchanged since the 1920s. However, it has been made less prominent over time.

The critical feature of the labour market is that while the owners of capital can choose whether or not to buy labour, those whose only asset is labour have no choice but to sell it. This imbalance of power is inherent in capitalism.

The ultimate goal of socialism and social democracy should be a society and economy where work is a choice rather than an economic necessity. A universal basic income would play a central role in such a society. It would imply, for everyone, the possibility of maintaining an adequate standard of living without market work.

For this to be a real choice, the other side of the coin is a job guarantee, to ensure that everyone who wants to work can work and earn a reasonable wage for doing so. The relationship between a UBI and a job guarantee is discussed by Fitzroy and Jin (2018), Quiggin (2018), and Henderson and Quiggin (2019).

Political obstacles

The political obstacles are substantial. The whole thrust of policy for decades has been to increase the intensity of work-testing for benefits of all kinds. And, unlike much of the neoliberal agenda, measures like 'work for the dole' have plenty of public support, despite the largely spurious nature of the work that can be required in such a scheme.

But the difficulty of the proposal is precisely the point. A UBI represents both a long-term challenge to the entire organisation of work and labour and, in the short term, a rallying point for a rejection of one of the central themes of neoliberalism, the critical importance of (paid) work. As the collapse of the neoliberal order accelerates under pressure from the political right, this mixture of utopian vision and immediate resistance is precisely what the left needs to offer.

It is not particularly challenging to take the first steps towards a UBI using a universal payment approach. This may be done through a relatively modest demogrant such as the Alaska Permanent Fund Dividend. However, as noted above, the next steps in the transition are more problematic. Transition to a UBI would require that the value of the universal grant should be increased over time. In reality, to cite the Alaskan example, the grant is an obvious source of potential savings when the budget comes under stress, and in Alaska, cuts have been proposed repeatedly.

Sustainability

Any discussion of the political sustainability of a full-scale UBI or guaranteed minimum income is obviously speculative. Not only has nothing of the kind ever been attempted, but the implied social transformation is so radical as to render analysis pure conjecture.

Nevertheless, longstanding arguments about the superior political viability of universalism compared to means-testing and targeting would seem to gain strength from the kinds of shifts required for such a policy.

As noted above, the difference between guaranteed minimum income and UBI is one of form rather than substance. Hence, once a basic income was universally available, or nearly so, it would be possible to restructure the system to convert it to a UBI.

How to get there

When fully implemented, UBI and guaranteed minimum income schemes are almost identical to each other (and to negative income taxes). To be more precise, in terms of the ultimate distribution of income and effective marginal tax rates, including the effects of means-testing basic payments, any UBI is equivalent to a guaranteed minimum income with the same guaranteed payment and similarly progressive taxes, and vice versa. For wage earners operating under the Pay-As-You-Earn system, there would be no difference in net pay, just a different way of calculating it on the payslip. Hence, if we actually achieved a genuine guaranteed minimum income, transforming it to a UBI would be largely a matter of definitions.

The critical question, then, is how to get there. Compared to the universal first approach, the basic first approach is of merit in that we are already part of the way there, and that the next steps involve clear and feasible political demands.

Bibliography

Brooks, James. 2017. 'Alaska House Votes to Lower Permanent Fund Dividend'. *Juneau Empire*. 12 April 2017. www.juneauempire.com/news/alaska-house-votes-to-lower-permanent-fund-dividend/.

Fitzroy, Felix, and Jin, Jim. 2018. 'Basic Income and a Public Job Offer'. *Journal of Poverty and Social Justice* 26, no. 2. doi.org/10.1332/175982718X15200701 225179.

Friedman, Milton. 1987. 'The Case for the Negative Income Tax'. In *The Essence of Friedman*, edited by Kurt Leube, 57–68. Stanford and Washington DC: Hoover Institution Press.

Henderson, Troy, and John Quiggin. 2019. 'Trade Unions and Basic Income'. In *Palgrave International Handbook of Basic Income*, edited by Malcolm Torry. Cham: Palgrave Macmillan. doi.org/10.1007/978-3-030-23614-4.

Leigh, Andrew. 2017. 'Why a universal basic income is a terrible idea'. Crikey.com. www.crikey.com.au/2017/04/21/universal-basic-income-terrible-idea/.

Lerner, Abba. 1943. 'Functional Finance and the Federal Debt'. *Social Research* 10, no. 1 (February): 38–51.

Quiggin, John. 2011. 'Money for nothing?'. *johnquiggin.com*. 18 October 2011. johnquiggin.com/2011/10/18/money-for-nothing/.

Quiggin, John. 2018. 'Labour market policy and the future of work'. In *Social Security Reform: Revisiting Henderson and Basic Income in Australia,* edited by Peter Saunders. Melbourne: Melbourne University Press.

Rhys-Williams, Julie. 1943. *Something to Look Forward to: A Suggestion for a New Social Contract*. London: MacDonald & Co. (Publishers) Ltd. doi.org/10.1057/9780230522824_16.

Torry, Malcolm. 2013. *Money for Everyone: Why We Need a Citizen's Income*. Bristol: Bristol University Press. doi.org/10.51952/9781447311263.

Van Parijs, Philippe, and Yannick Vanderborght. 2017. *Basic Income: A Radical Proposal for a Free Society and a Sane Economy*. Cambridge, MA: Harvard University Press. doi.org/10.4159/9780674978072.

Widerquist, Karl. 2013. 'What (If Anything) Can We Learn from the Negative Income Tax Experiments?' In *Basic Income: An Anthology of Contemporary Research,* edited by Karl Widerquist, José Noguera, Yannick Vanderborght, and Jurgen de Wispelaere. Chichester: Wiley Blackwell.

Widerquist, Karl. 2015. 'ALASKA, USA: 2015 Dividend Estimated to Be Near Highest Ever'. *The Basic Income Earth Network*, 31 August 2015. basicincome. org/news/2015/08/alaska-usa-dividend-amount-estimated-to-be-near-highest-ever/.

Widerquist, Karl, José Noguera, Yannick Vanderborght, and Jurgen de Wispelaere. 2013. *Basic Income: An Anthology of Contemporary Research*. Chichester: Wiley Blackwell.

Wright, Erik Olin. 2010. *Envisioning Real Utopias* (First Edition). London: Verso.

10

The case for a four-day standard working week

The five-day working week and the two-day weekend have been standard for so long that it is hard for many to imagine anything different. However, it dates back only to the middle of the 20th century as a normal way of working. Before that, Saturday was a normal working day in Western countries, and only Sunday was normally taken as a day of rest.

The advent of the weekend, and the associated standard workweek of 35 to 40 hours, was the culmination of a long series of reductions in working hours from the peak of 70 hours or more reached in the early 19th century (Schor 1993).

For most of the 20th century, it was expected that these reductions would continue, as technological progress reduced the labour input needed to produce any given volume of output. Writing in the 1930s, Keynes argued that a 15-hour week would be achievable in two generations, a claim assessed by Quiggin (2012). By the 1970s, substantial literature had been devoted to worrying about how people might manage to occupy all their free time (Jones 1982; Scitovsky 1976).

In reality, the trend towards reduced working hours came to a halt in the 1980s, ending with the shift to a 38-hour standard working week, as opposed to the 35-hour week unions had advocated since the early 1970s. Since then, there have been some improvements in parental and carers' leave but no general reductions in standard hours of work.

Meanwhile, the intensity of work has generally increased, and the dominance of the standard five-day week has been eroded by reductions in penalty rates. The result of these developments has been an increase in stress and burnout, with adverse consequences for both mental health and long-term productivity.

The experience of the COVID-19 pandemic has heightened concerns about stress and burnout. The problems have been particularly severe for front-line workers in health and aged care.

The pandemic has also overturned longstanding assumptions about the nature of work and our relationship to work. Most obviously, remote work has proved more successful than even its most optimistic advocates predicted. More generally, it has become clear that 'This is the way we've always done things' is not a sufficient basis for sticking to existing work arrangements.

One manifestation of this has been renewed interest in the idea of a four-day working week. A number of enterprises are undertaking trials as part of the 4 Day Week Global (4DW Global) initiative. These trials will provide useful evidence on how various versions of the four-day week might be implemented, and on the effects on mental health, work–life balance, productivity and job turnover.

While such individual initiatives are valuable, government action is essential. As major employers, governments can lead the way in implementing improved working conditions. And, at some point, the general shift to a four-day week will require legislative action.

A four-day working week is well within the realm of economic feasibility. But how much, if anything, would it cost in terms of lost production and lower wages?

History of working hours

In 1856, Melbourne stonemasons became some of the first workers in the world to achieve an eight-hour working day (New Zealand also claims this achievement). This event is still commemorated in Tasmania, where the Labour Day holiday is called Eight Hours Day.

For the 100 years and more following this milestone, standard working hours were slowly but steadily reduced. The working week was cut from six days to five by 1948, bringing us that great boon, the weekend. Thanks to steady increases in productivity, all this was achieved while living standards even improved steadily.

Although the standard work week remained fixed at five days, increases in leisure continued until the late 20th century. Annual leave was introduced, increasing to four weeks a year in the 1970s. Sick leave, long service leave and an increased number of public holidays all reduced the number of hours worked per year.

Finally, weekly working hours were cut from 40 to 38 in 1981. Some unionised workers in industries such as construction were able to negotiate slightly shorter hours, allowing them to work a nine-day fortnight. This typically involves working days of about eight hours for a total of 72 hours a fortnight, or 36 hours in an average workweek. That is the same hours per day as in the 19th century but with around two-thirds as many days of work in a year.

All this progress came to a halt with the era of micro-economic reform (often called neoliberalism) that began in the 1980s. There has been no significant reduction in standard hours since then. The actual number of hours worked has ebbed and flowed according to the state of the labour market, but without any clear trend.

A large increase in women's participation in the workforce was accompanied by an increase in part-time and casual employment. To some extent, the rise of part-time work allowed for an element of work–life balance consistent with traditional gender roles that assigned women more responsibility for home production and child care. However, the insecurity of casual employment worked in the opposite direction.

The industrial relations system

For most of the period of neoliberalism, employers favoured longer hours of work for their core full-time workforce, while workers and unions pushed for better work–life balance. The forces have ebbed and flowed, with no clear direction. No sustained progress towards improved work–life balance has been achieved since the 1990s.

In the 1990s, following the recession of 1989–91, bargaining power was strongly in the hands of employers. Work intensification resulted in a temporary increase in productivity, described at the time as a 'miracle', portending the emergence of a New Economy. This euphoria was short-lived (Quiggin 2001).

The intensity of work increased to the extent that conservative prime minister John Howard described the issue as a 'barbecue stopper' (Hewett 2001; quoted in Treguer 2023). Howard meant that mention of the issue was sufficient to stop discussion of any other topic. However, the increasing prevalence of unpaid overtime, including on weekends, meant that work intensification literally stopped barbecues from happening.

Improvements in the labour market contributed to a gradual reduction in the long hours of work from the late 1990s until the advent of the Howard government's *Workplace Relations Amendment (Work Choices) Act 2005* (WorkChoices), which again shifted the balance of power to employers. However, the balance shifted once more with the defeat of the Howard government in 2007, partly due to the 'Your Rights at Work' campaign led by the Australian Council of Trade Unions (ACTU).

Most recently, the experience of the COVID pandemic has made it clear that existing ways of organising work are not set in stone. Most notably, many workers found they could achieve better work balance through remote work, without any reduction in productivity. Strenuous efforts by managers and employers to impose a return to office-based work have been at most partially successful. More enlightened employers have accepted the need to accommodate change and allow workers more control over their lives.

The COVID experience has produced a variety of responses, including increased resistance to overwork ('quiet quitting') and greater job mobility ('The Great Resignation'). This in turn has increased the willingness of employers to consider ideas such as the four-day week, with the aim of improving worker satisfaction.

Work–life balance, burnout and employee retention

Work–life balance

Material standards of living have improved substantially over the past 40 years. By contrast, there has been no improvement in work–life balance.

If anything, the demands faced by Australian families outside working hours have been intensified. Social expectations about the need for parents to spend time with children have increased, and this is reflected in a global upward trend (Ortiz-Ospina 2020). The trend is particularly evident for university-educated parents, a group that is growing in size.

Technological progress has done little to offset this. Labour-saving devices, including refrigerators, washing machines, vacuum cleaners and microwave ovens, led to a considerable reduction in the hours required for housework from the 1950s onwards. However, most of the gains had been realised by the late 1970s, just as reductions in standard working hours came to an end.

The lack of progress in work–life balance is connected to a variety of social problems. For example, a survey by Relationships Australia (2008) found that stress and work pressures were among the primary obstacles to forming relationships and the primary external reasons for relationship breakdown.

Over the last decade or so, awareness of the problems has increased. A variety of responses have been tried, with the aim of increasing flexibility for workers and reducing burnout. However, without a reduction in standard hours of work, the problem is essentially insoluble.

Burnout

Burnout is a state of emotional, mental, and often physical exhaustion brought on by prolonged or repeated stress. Although burnout arises in a number of contexts, including parenting, it is most often caused, or at least contributed to, by problems at work.

Long hours are not the sole source of burnout, but they are commonly a contributing factor.

Burnout leads to mental health problems for workers, and poor work performance and high rates of resignation for employers. Although many employers are aware of the problem, it has historically proved difficult for individual employers to break from well-established, even if harmful, industry practices (Buchanan and Wanrooy 2001).

Collie (2015) notes the adverse consequences:

> Musculoskeletal conditions, traditionally the major type of workplace injury, are becoming less prevalent, whereas work-related mental health conditions are becoming more common. We have more workers with insecure jobs, we work longer hours on average, and workplace stress has been growing.
>
> But while we have been effective at reducing workplace risk for physical injuries in Australia, we have not paid the same attention to risk factors for mental health conditions.

Employee retention

It is widely recognised that burnout and overwork contribute to job turnover, and particularly to the loss of the skilled and motivated employees most likely to suffer burnout. Staff who are unable or unwilling to leave may adopt the option of 'quiet quitting', seeking to minimise their effort while maintaining an appearance of commitment.

Health and aged-care workers

Even before the COVID pandemic, healthcare workers such as nurses and doctors experienced high levels of stress and burnout. As Duckett and Meehan (2022) observe, citing Markwell and Wainer (2009):

> Multiple Australian studies have found burnout rates of more than 50 per cent among health care workers, although rates are lower in general practice. US surveys have also consistently shown burnout is higher among doctors, and especially emergency doctors, than in the general workforce.

A US study by Kronos Inc. (2017) found that more than three out of five nurses (63 per cent) say their work has caused job burnout, and two out of five (41 per cent) state they have considered changing hospitals in the past year because they have felt burned out.

More generally, any workplace that is characterised by stress and overwork is ill-placed to handle an emergency. If the health system had more workers on shorter standard hours, the capacity to handle a surge of demand through extra shifts would be much greater.

The resurgence of interest in the four-day week

As disillusionment with the economic consequences of neoliberalism has grown, there has been a resurgence of interest in ideas like the four-day week. The GFC was an important element in this process, undermining faith in markets, particularly in financial markets, which had always led the push for market reform.

The disruption created by the COVID-19 pandemic has led many of us to reconsider our relationship to work, as well as our priorities in expenditure. Some are eager to return to pre-pandemic 'normality'. Others have found working from home to be liberating and are keen to preserve some of their new-found autonomy. Still others, such as health workers, are simply exhausted after two years dealing with the ever-changing demands of the pandemic. One manifestation of our exhaustion has been the rise of the 'anti-work' movement, which rejects the whole idea of paid employment as a way to organise necessary labour.

A less radical response has been increased interest in the idea of a four-day working week.

What would a four-day working week look like?

Proposals for a four-day week differ regarding the associated change in working hours. At one extreme, some proposals leave weekly hours unchanged, compressing five days' work into four. At the other, daily working hours are unchanged, and the number of hours in the standard working week is reduced by 20 per cent. There seems little value in considering proposals with no reduction in weekly hours. With a 38-hour working week, and allowing an hour for lunch, that would entail 10.5 hours at work every day, with a commute potentially added. On the other hand, some increase in daily hours, such as a return to the eight-hour working day, might be an acceptable trade-off for a four-day week. This is discussed in more detail below, along with measures that affect leave arrangements of various kinds.

It is also necessary to consider whether a four-day week should take the form of a three-day weekend, extended to include Monday (or perhaps Friday). One alternative is an extension of the rostered day off prevailing in some parts of the building industry, where all workers have one day off each fortnight, but the number rostered on any given day is constant. Another option, derived from the experience of the pandemic, would be a core three-day week (Tuesday to Thursday) with workers having either Friday or Monday off.

One path to a four-day week

To provide a concrete basis for discussion, consider a proposal to replace the current standard working week of 38 hours over five days with a working week of 32 hours over four eight-hour days. The proposal would require both a reduction in annual hours of work and foregoing some existing entitlements (public and annual holidays).

The first step would be a reduction in the standard working week from 38 hours to 35 with no reduction in pay. Such a change was first proposed by ACTU in 1973, well before most current employees entered the labour force. In the subsequent period of nearly 50 years, GDP per hour worked has more than doubled, yet working hours have barely changed.

A reduction from 38 hours to 35 would be equivalent to an 8 per cent increase in real hourly wages. The cost to employers would be partly offset by the increase in output per hour commonly observed when standard working hours are reduced.

With four weeks' annual leave and 10 public holidays per year, a standard 35-hour working week would be equivalent to just over 1,600 hours of work per year, compared to over 1,800 hours at present. On the same basis, a 32-hour working week would be equivalent to just over 1,450 hours of work per year. However, with appropriate adjustments to leave and public holiday arrangements, a 32-hour working week would be consistent with 1,600 hours of work per year.

The first step would be to require four days of work on weeks that include a public holiday. In effect, public holidays would still be celebrated but would not produce a reduction in annual working hours. Under this adjustment, a 32-hour working week would be equivalent to just over 1,530 hours of work per year. Given that many public holidays exist primarily to provide workers with a long weekend, it seems unlikely that there would be strong objections to this trade-off.

The second, and probably more controversial, measure would be to reduce annual leave from four weeks to two for workers who chose to work a four-day week all year round. Workers who wanted four weeks of annual leave would be required to put in eight additional days of work during the standard working year. While this might sound complicated, it is similar to existing arrangements such as flexitime and days off in lieu of overtime.

A variation or extension of this proposal could be:

- Step 1: 35 hours
- Step 2: 32 hours with associated changes to public holidays and annual leave for those who 'choose' this option
- Step 3: 32 hours with a standard four weeks' annual leave but with provisions for working on public holidays retained.

The 4 Day Week Global trial

A variety of experiments with four-day weeks have been undertaken, but none have been particularly rigorous. The first large-scale trials are now being undertaken by 4 Day Week Global (4DW Global). The efforts of 4DW Global began with the adoption of a four-day week by New Zealand company trustee company Perpetual Guardian. This shift was highly successful and led to the establishment of 4DW Global, the aim being to provide credible evidence on the implications of a four-day week.

The approach adopted has been to seek the voluntary participation of employers and employees in a scientifically monitored trial. Experiments have commenced in a number of countries, including the UK and Australia. Participants complete questionnaires at the beginning and end of the experiment. The results are to be analysed by a team led by Professor Juliet Schor. The team includes Australian researchers Professor John Buchanan and myself.

At this point, the UK study has reached the halfway point. Survey data have yet to be completed and analysed. However, interim responses from employers have been highly positive.

A series of questions were posed. Participants choose each answer on a scale of 1 to 5. Of those who have responded:

- 88 per cent state that the four-day week is working 'well' for their business at this stage in the trial
- 46 per cent say their business productivity has 'maintained around the same level', while 34 per cent report that it has 'improved slightly' and 15 per cent say it has 'improved significantly'
- rating how smooth the transition to a four-day week has been, with '5' being 'extremely smooth' and '1' being 'extremely challenging', 29 per cent of respondents selected '5', 49 per cent selected '4' and 20 per cent selected '3'
- 86 per cent of respondents stated that at this juncture in the trial, they would be 'extremely likely' or 'likely' to consider retaining the four-day week policy after the trial period.

Summing up

Despite great technological advances and chronic concern over problems of work–life balance, Australian workers have seen no significant change in standard working hours for 40 years. The greatest barriers to change include inertia and the resistance of employers to reductions in working hours.

It is time to break through these barriers. The shift to remote work during and after COVID lockdowns has shown that radical change is socially and economically feasible.

Proposals for a four-day standard working week are now on the policy agenda. Progressive employers are already trialling various forms of the four-day week. It is time for governments to take the lead in this respect.

Bibliography

Buchanan, John, and Brigid van Wanrooy. 2001. *What About the Bosses? Employers and Extended Hours of Work: Insights from Exploratory Research.* Sydney: University of Sydney.

Collie, Alex. 2015. 'Dying for Work: The Changing Face of Work-Related Injuries'. *The Conversation*, 28 April 2015. theconversation.com/dying-for-work-the-changing-face-of-work-related-injuries-40328.

Duckett, Stephen, and Edward Meehan. 2022. 'How to Tackle Burnout Among Healthcare Workers'. *Croakey*, 23 March 2022. grattan.edu.au/news/how-to-tackle-burnout-among-healthcare-workers/.

4 Day Week Global. 2019. 'Guidelines for an Outcome Based Trial: Raising Productivity and Engagement'. White Paper 2019. www.4dayweek.com/access-white-paper.

Galanis, Petros, Irene Vraka, Despoina Fragkou, Angeliki Bilali, and Daphne Kaitelidou. 2021. 'Nurses' Burnout and Associated Risk Factors During the COVID-19 Pandemic: A Systematic Review and Meta-analysis'. *Journal of Advanced Nursing* 77, no. 8: 3286–302. doi.org/10.1111/jan.14839.

Hewett, J. 2001. 'Man on a Mission'. *Sydney Morning Herald*, 27 October 2001.

Jones, Barry. 1982. *Sleepers, Wake! Technology and the Future of Work*. Melbourne: Oxford University Press.

Keynes, John Maynard. 1930. 'Economic Possibilities for Our Grandchildren'. In *Essays in Persuasion*. New York: Harcourt Brace.

Kronos Incorporated. 2017. 'Kronos Survey Finds That Nurses Love What They Do Though Fatigue is a Pervasive Problem'. *Business Wire*, 8 May 2017. www.business wire.com/news/home/20170508005305/en/Kronos-Survey-Finds-That-Nurses-Love-What-They-Do-Though-Fatigue-is-a-Pervasive-Problem.

Lockhart, Charlotte. 2022. 'UK Companies in 4 Day Week Pilot Reach Landmark Halfway Point'. *4 Day Week Global*, 20 September 2022. www.4dayweek.com/press-releases-posts/uk-four-day-week-pilot-mid-results.

Markwell, Alexandra L., and Zoe Wainer. 2009. 'The Health and Wellbeing of Junior Doctors: Insights from a National Survey'. *Medical Journal of Australia* 191: 441–44. doi.org/10.5694/j.1326-5377.2009.tb02880.x.

Ortiz-Ospina, Esteban. 2020. 'Are Parents Spending Less Time with Their Kids?'. *Our World in Data*, 14 December 2020. ourworldindata.org/parents-time-with-kids.

Quiggin, John. 2001. The Australian Productivity Miracle: A Sceptical View. *Agenda* 8, no. 4: 333–48. doi.org/10.22459/ag.08.04.2001.04.

Quiggin, John. 2012. 'The Golden Age'. *Aeon*, 27 September 2012. aeon.co/essays/the-time-is-right-to-reclaim-the-utopian-ideas-of-keynes.

Relationships Australia and Credit Union Australia. 2008. 'Issues and Concerns that Australians Have in their Relationships Today'. *Relationships Indicators Survey 2008*. relationships.org.au/wp-content/uploads/ra-rel-ind-survey-2008-report.pdf.

Ramey, Valerie A. 2008. 'Time Spent in Home Production in the 20th Century: New Estimates from Old Data'. May 2008. Cambridge: National Bureau of Economic Research Working Paper 13985. doi.org//10.3386/w13985.

Sakzewski, Emily. 2021. 'The Burnout is "Absolutely Real": A Look at the State of Australia's Nursing Workforce amid Labour Shortage'. *ABC News*, 19 November 2021. www.abc.net.au/news/2021-11-19/australia-nurse-burnout-labour-shortage-supply-demand/100566430.

Schor, Juliet. 1993. *The Overworked American: The Unexpected Decline of Leisure*. New York: Basic Books.

Scitovsky, Tibor. 1976. *The Joyless Economy*. Oxford: Oxford University Press.

Tréguer, Pascal. 2021. '"Barbecue Stopper": Meaning and Origin'. word histories, 2021. wordhistories.net/2021/12/15/barbecue-stopper/.

Afterword

In the papers collected here, I have described and critically assessed various stages of the rise and decline of neoliberalism, beginning in the 1980s. In this afterword, I offer some brief updates.

On Chapter 1 White trash of Asia?: The dire warnings of the disaster that awaited us if we continued on our old path were a major driver of reform. Forty years after the 'White trash of Asia' scare, our regional neighbours have become much richer and Australia's share of regional income much smaller. We have also become a lot less white (on average) than we were then. Yet, none of the dire consequences predicted for us have come to pass.

On Chapter 2 The evolution of neoliberalism: For anyone who was not there at the time, it is hard to recapture the urgency and enthusiasm with which the neoliberal challenge to the economic institutions of mid-20th century Australia were greeted, at least by the majority of the political class. Looking back from the perspective of the present, the sense of disappointed hopes is palpable.

On Chapter 3 Neoliberalism in Australia: Those hopes were reflected in the title of my 1996 work *Great Expectations*. The focus on tariff protection in that book is a reminder that some of the issues that animated debate in the 20th century have become largely irrelevant with changes in economic structures. The industrial economy of the 20th century, with manufacturing at its core, has been replaced by an economy in which information services are central. With or without tariff reform, the decline of manufacturing in Australia was inevitable.

On Chapter 4 Privatisation and nationalisation in the 21st century: Among the failures of neoliberalism, privatisation has been the most striking. As I write this afterword, the New South Wales parliament has just passed legislation constitutionally enshrining the public ownership of Sydney Water. This is, admittedly, a piece of political theatre, since any prospect of privatisation has disappeared from the agenda. Nevertheless, it is indicative of the deep disrepute into which this policy has fallen. More substantively, we have seen the re-entry of public ownership in telecommunications with the National Broadband Network (NBN), and in electricity generation with the re-establishment of the State Electricity Commission of Victoria and similar moves in other states. Ideas like 'asset recycling' and BOOT (Build, Own, Operate and Transfer) have been thoroughly discredited.

On Chapter 5 Looking back on micro-economic reform: It is hard to recall now, but the term micro-economic reform was, when it was coined, an allusion to the then popular idea of supply-side economics. The point was to shift the focus of the economic debate away from macro-economic concerns about unemployment and inflation (demand-side economics) and towards enhancing the productivity of the economy by winding back government intervention. My restating of the view that macro-economic success (or failure) yielded larger and more sustained benefits (or costs) than micro-economic reform was largely ignored at the time. However, since the GFC, and even more since the advent of COVID-19, macro-economic issues have returned to centre stage. It seems unlikely that this will change any time soon.

On Chapter 6 What have we learned from the Global Financial Crisis?: As I argued in *Zombie Economics*, successful political ideologies have a life cycle of their own. They are born as fresh and exciting challenges to a failed status quo, then rise to dominate the debate before becoming 'common sense' conventional wisdom, just like the older ideas they displaced. Eventually, changes in conditions and weaknesses that have been overlooked prove fatal. But, even after death, they shamble on in zombie form. The lessons of the GFC are still sinking in. However, complete acceptance of those lessons may have to wait until policymakers whose ideas were fully formed before the crisis have departed from the scene.

On Chapter 7 The lost golden age of productivity growth?: The idea of a '1990s productivity miracle' has been forgotten by most. Nevertheless, debates over productivity continue to be plagued by measurement problems. The shift to remote work provides an important example. Reductions in commuting time represent an important increase in productivity, considered in economic terms. Yet, statistical measures of working hours do not include commuting times, so these gains are not measured.

On Chapter 8 Financial markets: masters or servants?: The most striking development is the way in which we think about the financial sector. In the 1980s and 1990s, financial sector operators were routinely described as the 'Masters of the Universe', bringing their power to bear to force irresponsible governments into fiscal probity. Now they are at best a necessary evil, too enmeshed in the system to be dispensed with but continuously creating crises of one kind or another.

On Chapter 9 Basic or universal? Pathways for a universal basic income and Chapter 10 The case for a four-day standard working week: The experience of the pandemic has made it clear that the ways we have done things during the 40 years of neoliberalism are not the inevitable result of objective needs and can be changed radically if we so choose. We have made some marginal steps towards a livable income guarantee with the first increases in the real value of unemployment benefits since the 1990s. Nevertheless, the idea remains on the margins of the policy debate. By contrast, interest in a four-day working week is growing all the time. It seems likely that a shorter standard working week will become common over the next few years. It could become a legal norm in the next decade or so.

***

The era of neoliberalism is over, but it is too early to say what will replace it. Both utopian and apocalyptic futures seem possible. My hope is that the work presented here will make a small difference in favour of utopia.

Index

Note: Page numbers with 'n' indicate footnotes.

reform
definition 5n4, 79
fatigue 59, 78, 134
regulatory risk 69, 73
relative growth 13, 14, 15, 18, 22–25
see also growth rates
remote work 2, 5, 6, 170, 172, 175, 178
see also COVID-19
renationalisation 64, 71–73
reregulation 84, 86
Reserve Bank of Australia 5, 85, 91, 108, 149
retirement income 145, 156, 157
see also age pension; universal basic income

Sanders, Bernie 28
sequencing 80
shock therapy, *see* radical restructuring
Singapore 9, 12, 13, 14, 17, 25, 51
social democracy 2, 27, 28, 29, 30, 31, 35, 37, 165
social democratic
era/moment 32, 42
ideas 31
parties 29, 30, 31, 36, 39, 40, 164
policies 33, 58
social security 32, 48n1, 158
see also unemployment, relief
social welfare 37, 38, 49, 53, 64, 145, 157
socialism 1, 30, 36, 53, 63, 64, 164, 164n5, 165
socialist objective 36, 53, 164, 164n5
Solow, Robert
residual/model 125, 126
South Sea Bubble 113, 141, 153
sovereign debt crisis 28, 109, 140, 144, 151
Soviet Union 36, 64, 80
Soviet bloc 39
stagflation 109

Standard & Poor's 142, 149
Stolper–Samuelson theorem 49
structural reform 80
superannuation 48, 48n1, 89, 156, 158
Sweden 10, 11, 13, 16, 111
Switzerland 10, 11, 15

tariff policy 21, 48, 52, 54, 57, 58
tax revolt (USA) 33, 56, 111
tax–welfare system 99, 159, 163
Taylor, John
Taylor rules 109, 118
technological progress/innovation 6, 14, 126, 127, 129, 153, 169, 173, 178
Telecom Australia 54, 82
see also Telstra
Telstra 70, 72, 73, 77, 85, 86, 87, 134
see also Telecom Australia
Thatcher, Margaret 2, 24, 33, 34, 79
Thatcher government 4, 63, 80, 111
Thatcherism 2
think tanks 33, 71, 118
Third Way 28, 30, 30n2, 36, 38
Tobin, James
Tobin tax 150, 151, 152
Trade Practices Act 1974 56, 88
Treasury view 115, 119
trickle-down economics 5, 110
triumphalism 35, 39, 63, 110, 142
Trump, Donald 4n3, 28, 41
Trumpism 4, 41, 42, 43
two-airlines policy 59, 59n6, 84, 85

unemployment 32, 55, 60, 83, 91, 93, 119, 119n2, 124, 140
measure of domestic wellbeing 24
older age 56
rates 16, 57, 90, 105, 106, 107
relief/benefits 49, 57, 158, 160, 161, 162–164

Milton Keynes UK
Ingram Content Group UK Ltd.
UKHW021053080824
446563UK00008B/465